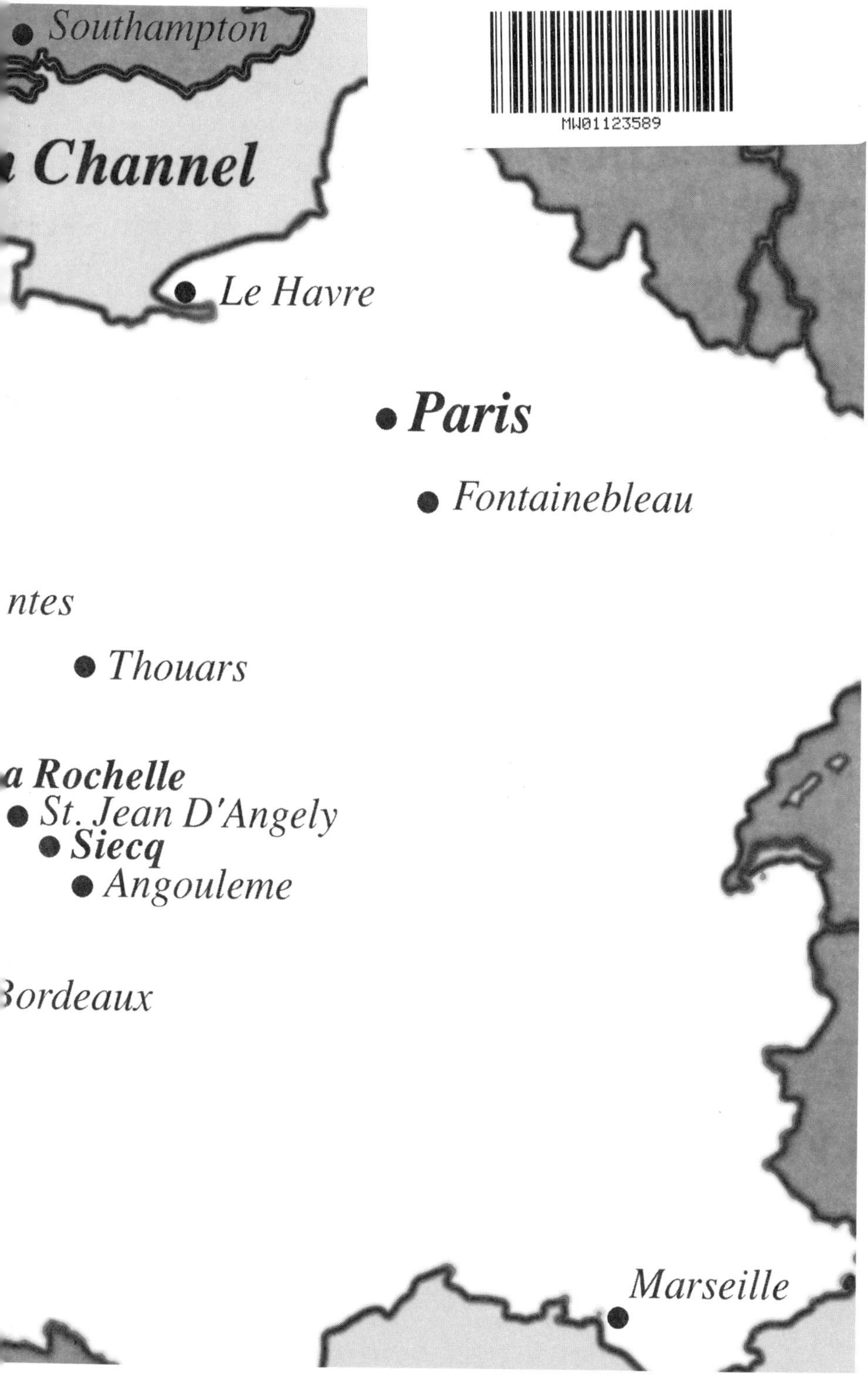
Southampton
Channel
Le Havre
Paris
Fontainebleau
ntes
Thouars
a Rochelle
St. Jean D'Angely
Siecq
Angouleme
ordeaux
Marseille

JOURNEYS TO FREEDOM

To
Rachel & Andy
I hope that you enjoy
this bit of the past —
[illegible]
5.19.07

JOURNEYS TO FREEDOM

A Compelling True Story of a Young Hungarian Born American Boy's Three Year Concealment from the Gestapo by French Supporters.

By

GUY GELLER

First Edition

ILREA PUBLISHING, Magnolia, Mississippi

JOURNEYS TO FREEDOM

A Compelling, True Story of a Young, Hungarian Born, American Boy's Three Year Concealment from the Gestapo by French Supporters

By Guy Geller

Published by:

ILREA Publishing
Post Office Box 123
Osyka, MS 39652-0123 U.S.A.

Library of Congress Cataloging Card Number

98-92981

ISBN 0-9663876-2-7

Printed and Bound in the United States of America, April 1998.

10 9 8 7 6 5 4 3 2 1

Journeys to Freedom, is dedicated to the memory of my father Gyula Geller, author, journalist and playwright. Would that he had survived the atrocities of Auschwitz beyond his thirty-fifth year to enjoy the fruit of his pen, in freedom.

This book is also dedicated to the real characters in this book without whose help, whether for ideology or financial gain, my journeys to our treasured freedom would never have been possible.

PERMISSIONS

Translated text of letters from G. Geller appearing on pages 8-9, 11-12, are from the library of Fereol de Gastyne and are printed with permission from Fed Services, Incorporated. ©1995

JOURNEYS

Preface

Had it not been for my children's thirst for family history and my desire to pass this legacy on to my grandchildren, this book may never have been written and the memories would have died with me.

It has taken fifty-five years to chronicle my father's disappearance, the daily bombing raids in France, the loss of playmates and the constant lookout for the Gestapo.

This story is not intended to compare Hitler's persecution of six million Jews who suffered atrocities of the Holocaust to my family's and my hardships. However, it does relate the experiences of a small boy, who, after losing his father to the Gestapo, prisons, concentration camp and finally the gas chambers of Auschwitz; is passed from link to link of an endless chain of sympathizers. They help him make his way to a destination that would keep him in hiding until the liberation of France and the end of World War II.

The next few chapters are a condensed narrative of the first ten years of his life in America. He travels from coast to coast six times, in search of a place he can call home.

Journeys to Freedom is written in thanksgiving to the dozens of people involved in my survival as well as that of hundreds of children like me.

Chapter One

It was a shortcut!

"Go to the *Metro*, down the steps and come up at the Molitor side. Go seven streets and you will be at the corner of *Rue de la Tourelle,*then you'll know where you are!"

Jacques had been telling me about that short cut for over a month. I knew that I should listen; after all he was at least a year older than me, therefore much wiser. He was the only other boy in an all girl Catholic school. Jacques and I discussed our situation from time to time asking Sister Marie Therése why there were no other boys in school. Each time she raised her eyes to the heavens with her hands clasped as if seeking guidance from above, she would then utter unintelligible words that we took to mean, "Go away, I can't tell you".

October 13th, 1942 was my father's thirty-fifth birthday. I wanted to hurry home to give him the card that I had made that day. I decided to walk with Jacques to the *Metro*. I promised myself that I would listen to his directions carefully. He would then go his way and I, following his instructions, was sure to arrive home much faster than usual.

A birthday party was out of the question. Food in 1942 Paris was extremely scarce. We had to form queues for hours just to buy our weekly ration of rutabaga, the staple that we had been eating boiled and mashed for over six months. Occasionally we were able to find one or two high priced potatoes. Maman saved the peels to make soup.

My mother had many talents. She had studied art at the Sorbonne, painted beautifully and played the piano. She had published a few stories of her own and had worked with my father while he wrote a number of theater pieces, but with all that she had never excelled in the culinary arts. Well, no matter, more important, we would be together.

Jacques and I set out at four o'clock. We ran down the *Metro* steps; he pointed me in the right direction, waved and went his way. I waved back, not knowing that this would be our farewell.

As I emerged from the white tiled walls of the Metro onto the street, I looked around and saw nothing familiar. Apprehension swept over me! Jacques had said "Go seven blocks and you will be on *Rue de la Tourell*e." There were four ways to go those seven blocks. I chose one, went two blocks. Still nothing looked familiar! I retraced my steps, looked around and headed in the direction that I felt sure would take me home. I half walked and half ran, recording each of the seven blocks on my fingers. I looked up at the blue and white street sign and saw *Tourelle*. It didn't look right. I looked more closely, my earlier apprehension turned to panic. I read *Court des Tourelles.* It was getting late; normally I would have been home by now. I had no idea where I was. I looked around hoping to find a friendly face.

Late on a cold autumn afternoon during the German occupation there was not another person on the street. I walked another block away from Court des Tourelles. Then I saw a hunched figure across the street, a woman heavily bundled against the chill was coming my way. I crossed the street, ran up to her and exclaimed, "*Pardon Madame- Je suis perdue*!" (Excuse me Madame- I am lost!).

She looked at me and with irritation in her voice asked where I was going. As an afterthought she asked my age. "I am six years old and I have to find *Rue de la Tourelle.*" Her voice softened somewhat, she took my hand and walked with me. We wound our way right and left in more turns than I would have imagined, but the blocks were not square. After the last series of turns the big house with the iron fence surrounding it loomed ahead in the near twilight, our apartment was only three houses away.

I sighed in relief and told my guide that I knew where I was. I thanked her politely for the guidance as she patted my head and gave my shoulder a gentle push in the direction of our house.

I broke into a trot, my mind racing. All at once my bare legs felt cold. It had started to drizzle, and now I was afraid that I would be punished for being late. I thought of Jacques and his short cut. I thought of the card that I had drawn for my father's birthday. Yes, it was still in the leather book satchel he had made for me.

Finally, I arrived at number 24. I rang for the concierge to release the lock on the heavy wrought iron and glass door. Nothing happened. I rang again and again. Still nothing!

The man from the ground floor apartment was just walking up, key in hand. He unlocked the door, looked at me and held the door open. I had always been petrified of him. The scar on his left cheek made his eyebrow droop and the corner of his mouth come up in a constant grimace. His collection of swords, spears and shields on his walls added to my fears.

My father had told me that German students frequently had saber scars on their faces; it was a badge of honor. I worked up the courage to walk past him, recalled my good manners, and thanked him. I scurried up the short flight of stairs to our first floor apartment. I was too young to have a key, so I rang the bell; then knocked on the door. I called for Papa to let me in. I knew that my mother would not be home from her work until much later. I turned around, looked at the cold, cream colored marble of the foyer and sat on the top step's red carpet runner.

The concierge almost always stayed in her apartment. I decided to walk down the steps and knock on the door. The door opened just a crack. I saw the lady put her hand to her mouth as she exclaimed *"mon Dieu!"*. The same hand snaked down, grabbed my arm and quickly pulled me into the smoke filled room. Her husband was reading a book, smoking a cigarette. A blue pack of *Gauloises* lay on the table next to a glass of *gros rouge*. (At least that was what Pepére, my grandfather Feréol called it.)

We had lived in that apartment a little over a year. Our second Christmas was coming soon. The only time I had ever seen them was during an earlier air raid. At the sound of an air raid siren all residents were to descend to the storage cellar and remain in their designated area. Chicken wire and thin boards separated each cubicle. Usually, though, we stood in the stairway listening to the adults discussing our fate with our neighbors.

I had never spoken to the *concierge*, or to her husband. I didn't even know their names. She sat me down on a chair full of cushions and shawls and put a cup of scalding hot bouillon in my hands. They both went into the other room. Low murmurs quickly turned into loud bickering. I overheard the dreaded word "Gestapo". Then he said loudly that "*le gosse*" couldn't stay. She seemed to put up a little argument, but the next thing I knew I was being escorted back out to the steps. I asked about my father. All they said was *"Il nes pas la!"* (He is not there).

I sat there for what seemed an eternity. I had no idea what time it was. I was cold in my short pants, sandals and gray school smock. At last, my mother came home from her office. We went in, and immediately she knew that something was drastically wrong.

My father stayed in the house almost all the time, since he was hiding from the Germans. He would write his plays and theater pieces. I found it strange that for newspaper articles he would use the *nom de plume*, Gerard Sylvain. Then he would read a lot. Often times after school I would sit on a tall stool for hours watching him paint small flowers and Hungarian scenes on glass trays and vases. He entertained me by telling me of Hungary where I was born, of the farms that belonged to my other grandfather, Nayapa and of the three beautiful hotels " Palatinus, the Palace and the Astoria" that belonged to my Great Uncle Mishka. All those, he said would someday be mine. He talked about my Aunt Anne, his sister and her husband Karoly, whose name I had been given as my middle name. He spoke of the big factory that they owned outside of Budapest and that they had no children.

On special days Papa would bind books beautifully in leather. All the neighbors knew when he was binding. The horse hoof glue would emit a horrible stench when it was heated on the kitchen burner. Generally the only time he went out was for us to make an occasional trip to the market or to take me to the *Bois de Boulogne.*

The way to the market was by the *Picine Molitor*. The large glass windows allowed me to feed my fascination by watching the people diving and swimming. One day I was so busy looking through the window that I walked right into an iron light standard. Immediately my father placed the cold buckle of his briefcase on the bump on my head to keep the swelling down. I was very proud,

I didn't cry. We were aware of another outing, his weekly meetings not far from our apartment.

Now in distress maman telephoned their friends, the hospitals and finally the police stations searching for my father. There were no satisfactory answers for two or three days. Maman had to go to her office, and I was to go back to school on Friday. On Thursday I went to the big house behind the fence. The owners were friends of my parents; they had a daughter my age. The lady walked home with me that evening.

A black car with black Swastikas centered in white circles on red flags mounted on the front fenders was parked in front of the house. Looking up the short flight of stairs through the glass, we saw the open door to our apartment. We hesitated, but quietly tiptoed through the door and down the long hall, through my mother's bedroom onto her balcony. From there we could see Maman standing in my father's study, flanked on either side by a uniformed German soldier. An officer dressed in the black uniform of the "SS" was searching my father's carved ebony desk. My father was so proud of the desk and matching *bibliotheque*. They, like the rest of his study were an "extension of his good taste", my mother had said many times. The officer shuffled papers, read notes and seemed to ask a lot of questions. He found the metal box where my father always kept emergency money. It was an easy task for him to break the lock with my father's letter opener and then to pocket the money.

Next he asked my mother for the keys to the glass door library that contained my father's prized leather-bound books. She did not have the keys, so she told him that he would have to break that in the same way that he had broken into the desk. He seemed to resent the flip answer but also he apparently appreciated the beauty of the piece. He just looked at the titles, shook his head and told her that she could be arrested simply for having those books in her house.

Apparently they had already searched my mother's room where we crouched, hidden. There did not seem to be much more that they would do at that time. Before they were to leave, Maman asked the "SS" officer in German what happened to my father. He stood at attention and said, "Your husband was arrested on October 13th at two o'clock at the home of some people who had summoned him for a meeting. He is now in jail and you will never see him again. As for you and your sons we will study your cases and we will come back later with a decision".

When the Germans departed, the neighbor left me alone with my mother, chilled and terrified. Maman was sitting down with her head in her hands, massaging her temples as she often did, trying to decide how to find my father.

A friend of maman, Mademoiselle Henriette came over the next morning, and they decided that they would split up on their bicycles and go to different prisons in and around Paris to try to find my father.

Mademoiselle Henriette was the one who found out that he was at the "Fort de Romaiville." She was unable to see him, but she was told that he could receive packages from home that could not exceed two kilograms. Maman quickly assembled some clothing, towels and a little medicine to make up a parcel so that he would know that we had found him. She searched in vain for any type of food to add to the package.

We had hoped that he would be released soon; undoubtedly there had been a mistake. However, if for some reason he was not to be released, we had thought that he would stay at the "Fort de Romainville" through the winter.

Soon after, we received a card from him saying that he would be transferred from where he was but could not tell us where he was to be sent.

A couple of days later we received a letter smuggled out by someone who had been released.

October 1942.

By another indirect way as dangerous as the first time, I am forwarding this hasty note that will not tell you all the love I have for you.

You must know that in this very tragic period of my destiny there are only affectionate thoughts and faithful attachments, which I regret, I was unable to show you lately.

Never forget that I keep your picture in my heart that will beat for you and our sons until the very last. Be their mother as I would have liked to stay their father and I will be able to accept this undeserved misery with courage and confidence.

Gather yourselves together - the three of you-and never part one from the other, never, so you do not know the tearing and horror of the absence which is my real torture. The rest is a man's destiny...

You must as soon as you receive this, the same as for the first letter, destroy it immediately, without any trace left because these two messages are going out without permission!!! If you were not able to find out yet the place of my actual internment, it is the Fort de Romainville, near the Porte des Lilas. You must ignore it whatever happens. If by some authorized way you hear of where I am, consider the notes as a simple testimony of my constant thoughts.

If you have not heard of my residence, do not come to this fort by yourself because you would be asked how you know it. Send one of your friends, Henriette, and she could say that being without any news from me you are trying to find out everywhere.

I need some warm clothes, a blanket, food, toilet articles, something to sew with and medicine. Put it all in a duffel bag. Try to find through the Quakers (who I hear can take care of these parcels). But please! Be very careful, be prudent!

I really do not know why I am here nor how long I am going to be here, also what is my destiny... If I could be reassured regarding the children's fate and yours, all the rest would seem easier.

I send my love to everyone we love and I kiss you with all the warmth of my heart.

I just heard now that tomorrow we are moving to Compiegne. Wait for news. *G.*

We then received a censored letter asking for heavy clothing. Officially he was allowed to send two cards and one letter per month. Immediately we thought that he was going to be sent somewhere in the East, Germany or worst, Poland!

Before the war my father's uncle had wanted him to train to take over the management of the hotels, so Papa had spent several months in Switzerland studying management at the best hotel school in Europe. He had kept his heavy woolen winter clothing. Maman made a large parcel. This time she went to the black market to buy tins of sardines, cakes and even vitamins. She sent him our week's ration of bread. Maman made him a sewing kit from one of her dresses and a small bag with drawstrings from my pajamas, the ones with the little teddy bears I had worn often while he told me my nightly bed time story. She hoped they would remind him that the entire family loved him. She enclosed his silver travel razor, writing paper, pencils, a French dictionary and his Bible.

Maman had not received another visit from the Gestapo as had been threatened on the evening of the fifteenth. The situation was getting worse in and around Paris. Air raid sirens screeched almost nightly. Bombings were more frequent and we heard about more Jewish friends being arrested for no reason. The Vichy government police working with the German military also arrested many of the non-Jews who were helping them. It was almost as it had been on July thirteenth when thirteen thousand Jews had been arrested and taken to the Velodrome d'Hiver. From there they had been transferred to a camp at Drancy to await departure to points east.

It was during that time, that Maman found out that my father had been involved with a group of twelve people who smuggled Jews out of Paris to England and to South America. The newest member of the group turned out to be a spy. He had informed the Germans, who had him request a special important meeting. The day of the meeting the Gestapo raided the house, arrested everyone present, even the informer. We never learned of his fate, though he was probably released.

I had gone back to school. The moment I arrived I looked for Jacques to tell him about his short cut, but he was not there. I asked the sister if he was sick; this time again, her eyes rolled to the heavens, but there was no answer.

The first week in December we received another smuggled letter dated November 30th 1942.

November 30th, 1942

My Dear, Day before yesterday I received the parcel with the clothes. Thank you with all my heart! The objects are very precious and I can imagine all the sacrifices you are going through to have made such a beautiful parcel! You certainly understand its utility. So now I am dressed for a long winter and if I have to undertake a big trip towards the East (everyone speaks about it all the time, saying I will never see you again if I go), I shall have less fear of the rigors of the weather! But if I have to stay here long before an uncertain freedom comes, I still never give up hope. These clothes just received will have considerable importance in a sojourn which is not made of delights. In unpacking the parcel so beautifully done, in opening the duffel bag from which each object gives me joy, the few men who were beside me could not help congratulating me and complimenting me for having such a wife whose fairy fingers have left their trace everywhere. The sewing bag is so complete and pretty! Why did you send me your lovely silver embroidery scissors that you like so well? I know that you have had them all your life. I am really sorry to have taken them away from you. The medicine was so carefully picked out. It all speaks of you with more adulation than I could write if I filled pages. I do not want to even mention all the new things you bought. I am sad for all the effort you made to find them, and happy at the same time for all your self sacrifice and devotion to me. Once more I thank you and I am deeply appreciative.

I still wait for your second letter, also the third. Please do not send any more registered mail unless very important, because everyone notices, and I do not want to make myself conspicuous. I do hope that they have not deprived me of some of those letters.

Write to the Commandant of the Camp, in German, and ask him if he will permit you to come visit me. If I were to stay here, he might allow you to come after a few months and maybe you will bring Guy along. If it is God's will you will succeed. I shall keep praying for your visit.

Do not speak to Guy about it, but I cannot give up all hope of seeing him once again. I am all confused! I do not know what is best. I am so afraid for my little boy to see me in prison. What would he think and feel? I want to leave it for you to decide, if such happiness is given to me to see you once again.

Sometimes I think about my return to you. One day a door will open in front of me, a door all white, from which I have lost the key; and behind that door will be my wife with her two sons. Each one will have a smile of welcome for me... I am so powerless! More than a blind man amputated of his legs and arms. I can only hope and wait. In this loss of civil rights which is my lot along with thousands and thousands of energetic men who are willing to act, even in this loss of freedom. It is not so much the trampling of our human dignity that is the most terrible to stand, but the powerlessness imposed upon us, consuming our will like rust. Once again I want to tell you of my deep appreciation for your beautiful attitude, and I keep touching the little pieces of material with the flowers from your dress also from Guy's pajamas. *Love, G.*

Maman telephoned Sister Marie Therése to tell me to go to the neighbor's house after school. Later another friend would come to get me. I was to go with her to spend the night.

Almost three hours after I arrived at the neighbor's house the buzzer at the front door sounded. An attractive lady wearing an open trench coat looked around as she entered. She saw me, held out her hand not as in a handshake but with the palm down, beckoning me to join mine with hers. That motion opened the folds of her coat just enough for me to see the yellow Star of David with a bold "*Juif*" embroidered in the center. She almost smiled and said that she was Doctor Eva and that I was to go with her. Last names were seldom used in those days. My mother would not be home for a few days, so she had asked her to take me with her.

Chapter Two

We walked past our apartment that I wouldn't see again for almost four years. I was dressed the same way I had been when I left for school that morning. By then it was really cold. Dr. Eva opened her coat and flipped the right tail around me. Her body warmth helped and the coat kept the wind away from me except for my legs. I was used to the chill.

I remember standing in line at the creamery in my short pants with my aluminum milk can, waiting my turn to get the half-liter of skimmed milk. My ration was available only when the shopkeeper took pity on me, which was not very often. Two or three times a week she used the ruse that there had not been a delivery. Everyone knew that in reality the milk went either to her friends or more likely to the black market. Disappointed, I would walk the eight or ten blocks home, often with snow over my shoes and past my ankles. The next scheduled time I returned with the hope of filling my can. Then I walked back home, went back out in the opposite direction to go to my school.

It was pitch black. Parisians were ordered to observe the black out under penalty of imprisonment. We walked for what seemed like hours. It was awkward walking at first. I kept stumbling. Dr. Eva told me to wrap my arm around her leg. This would make it easier to walk, and I would not come from under her coat and be cold. We tried it that way. She was tall but not tall enough for me to wrap my arm around her leg without hunching down a little.

I tried to ask her questions about my father; about where we were going and what would happen to my mother since the police and the Gestapo were coming back to our house. Dr. Eva told me that she was a friend of my father and that my mother knew I was with her and for me not to worry. Other than that she knew nothing. It turned out the "SS" and the French police had returned. They asked Maman for her papers and my birth certificate. She said that she could not find the birth certificate but she could show them my baptismal certificate. They saw that my name was not the same as my brother's but it was the same as my father's whom they had imprisoned. They seemed to be satisfied for the instant, they did not arrest my mother, but they told Maman that they were interested in me and would be back.

Fortunately Maman had gone to the *"Commissariat General aux Questions Juives"*, presented her papers and received a *"Certificat de Non-Appartenance a la Race Juive"*. a certificate satisfying the authorities that she appeared not to be Jewish.

COMMISSARIAT GÉNÉRAL AUX QUESTIONS JUIVES

2,571

CERTIFICAT
DE NON-APPARTENANCE A LA RACE JUIVE

Sur le vu des pièces produites par l'intéressée le Commissaire Général aux Questions Juives constate que Mme Geller née Erraudeau Louise
née le 3 mai 1903 à Cahors (Lot)
ne doit pas être regardée comme juive aux termes de la loi du 2 Juin 1941.

Paris, le 19 novembre 1942

Dr. Eva speaking in a loud whisper told me not to talk until we reached her house. The events of the last few days went through my mind. They had really been "difficult days" as my mother called them. I didn't remember having had any really "difficult days" before. Well maybe one, there was the day that my father had caught me lying about smoking seven cigarettes that my older brother Serge had convinced me to smoke. My hands had been behind my back when he asked if I was smoking. I told him no, though he could see the plume of smoke rising from behind my head. That was the only time that I can remember receiving a spanking. His displeasure would have been as demoralizing to me as the spanking. He was stern but gentle and loving. Papa made it very clear that though he was totally against smoking, the spanking was for lying about it.

We walked to the "Place de la Porte D'Auteuil". I recognized it since my father and I had been there several times during our walks to the Bois de Boulogne. From there we made so many turns that I lost track of where I was.

At last Dr. Eva stopped in front of a tall, dark green double door, looked around, unlocked it and pushed me in. An oil lamp burning on the drain of the kitchen sink emitted a dim yellow light. The kitchen was really an alcove off the large room we had entered. She closed the door, locked it and then slid the large squeaky bolt home and placed a heavy chair under the ornate doorknobs.

Instead of turning on the electric lights she lit another lamp, walked to the lone window on the street side of the room and adjusted the blackout curtain that probably did not need adjusting. She looked at me, shook her head from side to side, saying over and over "*Pauvre petit*". She walked over to where I stood bewildered, knelt on the floor, gathered me in her arms and quietly began sobbing. I stood stiff as a board, not knowing what to do while her emotions flowed. I was in a strange house with a strange woman who said that she was a doctor and a friend of my father and all was going to be well. I was not convinced since she was on her knees in front of me crying. Some time later, in retrospect, I wondered if the tears were for me, for circumstances, or perhaps for a desperate, secret love of my father.

She shook off the melancholy, then helped me out of my school smock, my short pants and my shoes. The apartment consisted of a large room with a bed and a sofa bed and a small alcove for a kitchen. There was no heat. I stood there in my briefs, not knowing what to expect, thinking that I should run. She stood up and gently pushed me to the sofa bed. In a continuous motion she turned the spread back and pushed me into bed. I was then given instruction to turn toward the wall and not to look toward her bed. I did as I was told.

Curiosity got the better of me. I opened my eyes looking toward my feet and saw Dr. Eva's reflection in a full-length cheval mirror as she undressed preparing for bed. I didn't remember having seen anything quite like that before. Dr. Eva removed all her clothes as I watched in the mirror. At one time I thought that she looked at me, but my head was in the shadows and I quickly closed my eyes. I was sure that I had not been caught. She walked to the kitchen to blow out the lamp. I heard her climb into bed and blow out the last lamp.

Mon Dieu it was dark I thought again. I was lost in my own world re-living the past few weeks. The bombing! We all tried to appear strong, but we were terrified. Almost each day after an air raid we heard that someone we knew had been wounded, mutilated or killed. I thought of an experience at the bakery. I had walked through the front door as usual. This time there was no smell of fresh bread. I looked up and saw no roof. Feathery smoke in back of the bakery reached for the low hanging clouds as if trying to rejoin the mother cloud.

The baker was sitting on the floor behind the counter. I could see the top of his bald head as he swayed back and forth crying. Hesitantly, I walked to the edge of the counter, peeked around at him holding his wife's head in his arms rocking. I stared for a second before the realization struck me. Only the torso was attached to that head; from the waist down, there was nothing but blood. My stomach churned, and my head spun. I managed to will the horrible tasting bile back down as I turned and ran. Had I eaten in the previous three days I might have just let it come up. I picked my way through the spider web of fire hoses that had appeared in the short time that I was in the store. I remember yelling unintelligible sounds to the top of my lungs all the way home.

Then I thought of an eight-year-old friend, Jean, who had lived across the court from us. On the days that my father was at his meeting and my mother was at work, I went to his apartment after school. He and I played for hours with his electric train.

A bomb landed on the house of relatives he was visiting. I never saw him again. I lay in bed wondering how many more friends I would lose to this terrible war. They were all children like me, simply wanting to grow up with our families. Now they would not even have a chance at life. I began to cry quietly.

I was brought back from my reveries by a strange noise from Dr. Eva's bed. She must have been turning over a lot trying to get comfortable, it was moving and squeaking. I thought, she too must have been dreaming. Soon all was quiet. My sobbing seemed deafening to me. She called for me to get into bed with her. I hurried across the short distance and quickly eased my thin body under the covers. She wrapped her arms around me. I can remember how soft, yet firm she felt to me. I cuddled as closely as I could before going to sleep.

I awoke, opened my eyes and realized that I was in a strange bed in a totally strange place. Panic struck me until through the glow of a candle across the room, I recognized the now somewhat familiar Dr. Eva. She was squeezing the handle of a stove lighter repeatedly, not even getting a spark. Exasperated, she took the candle and used it to ignite the two-burner gas stove. She had left the gas on throughout her attempts, the gas ignited with a "whoosh" driving her back a step. She half-stumbled, muttering *"merde"* under her breath. She was making what passed for Parisian coffee; ground dark roasted barley. She looked over at me and smiled. "You slept well!" she said. I guessed that I had because I did not remember anything after going to sleep. She told me to get dressed to fend off the chill. I pulled the only clothes I had under the covers to warm them before dressing, then sat on the side of the bed hesitating to move.

She motioned me to the small table between what served as the kitchen and the bedroom. She poured a bowl of "coffee", placed it in front of me and emptied the remains of her milk can into it. She then broke up the rest of a dried *"baguette"* in my bowl and into her large cup.
I asked if she had any children, since only people with children could have a ration of milk.

Dr. Eva looked at me very seriously, ignored my question, and then told me that it was six thirty and she had a long walk to her work. I was to stay inside until she returned around three thirty.

I stayed in the apartment as I had been instructed. I spent the first hour looking through her many textbooks.

Some had drawings of skeletons, some of men and women showing muscle structure. That became pretty boring. I was the best reader in my class, and I had the weekly prizes to prove it, but I could not read well enough to keep myself entertained with adult books.

I lifted the blackout curtain and looked out of the window again; it was daylight but raining and dreary. Very few people were hurrying to work.

"When you are a guest or visitor in someone's house, leave things alone. Don't look in drawers or closets", was one of my father's cautions that came during one of his painting sessions.

Yet it certainly was tempting. He had not said anything about boxes, and there must have been at least a dozen of various sizes. Some were polished wood, others were carved, and there was even a small one made of ivory. I imagined the treasures that those boxes held. I picked one up and walked over to Dr. Eva's reading chair under the lamp with the red fringed shade. I started to open it but closed it back. I held it on my lap and wondered what I could do for the rest of the day. Nothing had been said about food for lunch. I closed my eyes briefly, thinking back over some of the facts my father had told me.

He had been born in Hungary, went to France in 1934 and became a French citizen in 1939. I had been told that he was a journalist, a music and literary critic. He had also written books and a few plays. I knew that he had written a book about the great actress Sarah Bernhardt, and that he and maman kept a large binder of newspaper clippings about the book. I knew that he had weekly meetings. He would say often that he had been with the General or with Maurice Rostand a fellow author, the son of the famous Edmond Rostand.

We had visited the General in his home once. He was an elderly, very distinguished looking retired French Army general from World War I. I knew him to be my brother's mathematics tutor.

Serge, my brother, really my half brother from one of my mother's previous marriages, was older by just over six years and was usually away at a *pension* forty kilometers outside of Paris in Fontainebleau. Though he was not too good at mathematics, some of my parents' friends said that he was a musical genius. By the time he was eight he had composed several pieces, at twelve he was sneaking into Notre Dame de Paris to play the huge organ. Strangely, no one chased him out until he had finished playing. I thought that he was the greatest until he got me in trouble because of the seven cigarettes.

The more I thought the more I felt sure that even though my father had been taken, they realized their terrible mistake and had released him. He must now be back and trying to find me. I got up, replaced the box and again walked over to the window. It had stopped raining. I looked out thinking that I would be able to find Papa if only I could get out of the house. Dr. Eva had told me to stay and wait for her. I usually did as I was told, but this was different. Some inexplicable force drew me.

I looked in her armoire and found a sweater that was much too big for me but it looked warm. I put it on, the sleeves hung down to my knees and it wrapped around me twice. I guess that I looked sort of strange but this was *pendant la guerre,* (during the war) a phrase that always seemed to excuse the adults for their actions.

I made up my mind, and went to look for him. He was not only my father, he was also my best friend and I missed him. I managed to unlock the door and open it. I closed the door behind me unable to lock it, looked both ways, took a deep breath, and turned left. When I reached the corner I looked at the street sign which was *Rue de la Fontaine*. I knew the name well; my father and I had read some of the fables "de la Fontaine" I guess the familiarity of it made going that way comfortable.

I remember taking a right on a large avenue and then ending up by the Seine. I walked to the bank, looked over the wall and there was the "Statue de la Liberté". I had seen it earlier that year when Boris, a Polish student friend of my mother had taken me to the Tour Eiffel. I knew that I didn't want to cross the river, for then I would certainly be lost.

I was preoccupied with my surroundings when all at once across the avenue from the riverbank I saw a man walking briskly away from me but in the same direction. He bowed his balding, bare head as he hunched his shoulders and turned up the collar of a tan colored raincoat, just like my father wore. We were both walking into the wind and the beginning of an icy drizzle. If only I could see his face. I had no hope of catching him walking so I broke into a run. My oversized sweater sleeve seemed to trip me every other step. I picked up the hem as if it were a skirt and started calling after him, "Papa, Papa." He didn't hear me. Finally I had a chance to cross the Avenue. My heart was in my throat and I was still yelling "Papa, wait for me". He seemed to hear me. He glanced back, then broke into a trot with his coat tails flying.

That split second of a glance had been enough for me. My stomach fell. I knew that I was following the wrong man. Tears welled into my eyes. I stopped running, and wiped my eyes with the back of my hand. Why did the man run? The coarseness of the sweater sleeve against my face brought me back to reality. I stood there for a few seconds, holding back tears of disappointment and despair.

Jerkily I looked around. I had done it again. I was lost! I tried to retrace my steps, but since I had been so sure that man was my father and all was going to be well, I didn't pay attention to landmarks or signs. I knew that I had walked on Rue de la Fontaine, but I had forgotten to look at the name of the street that Dr. Eva's house was on.

People were going into the few open bistros along the Avenue de Versailles. It must have been close to noon. I should have been hungry, but as a sign of the times our stomachs were not accustomed to regular meals, so we ate a little whenever there was the chance. I looked for a *gendarme*. I had not seen one in quite some time. It dawned on me that even if I found one I probably didn't want to talk to him. Rumor was that most of them were helping the Gestapo, so I really didn't know what I would say if I did find one.

The rain had started falling in earnest. I pulled the neck of the borrowed sweater over my head but it was soaked; the only thing it did was let water run down behind my ears and down my back. Adults wearing raincoats huddled under umbrellas. They looked at me as if I was a street urchin. Maybe at this time it was what I had become. I decided that I had to do something to get in from the rain and to ask for some kind of help. I walked into one of the *bistros*.

The red-faced waiter looked down at me and said very seriously, *"Un Pernod pour monsieur?"* I looked at him thinking that he could not be serious. There was now a half smile on his face as he bent down to ask where I lived. I told him that I was visiting my aunt, went out for a few minutes and became lost. I didn't know her address and my parents were out of town so I could not go home. As paying customers were coming in, my waiter quickly lost interest in me. He half asked and half told the pretty lady sitting at a small table by herself to see what she could do with me. She jumped up shouting that she knew it was going to become her responsibility. They bantered back and forth jovially at first, then serious words were exchanged, the gist being that neither wanted to take the time to care for me. She would miss some work and his customers were very demanding.

I was thinking that I should leave. I certainly didn't want to cause problems and definitely didn't want to attract more attention than I already had. One look outside and I tried to find a way to postpone my departure. Though I was ill at ease inside, at least there,it was not raining.

I must have looked pretty pitiful because Mademoiselle Colette, she told me her name, came over, took my hand, brought me back and sat me down at her table. She went through the same questions the waiter had asked of me, but I was still unable to give her the address. Of course Colette's next question was my aunt's name. I told her that it was Eva but I couldn't remember her last name. *"C'est parfait"* Colette said to no one in particular, rolling her eyes and throwing both hands in the air. She reached across the table and in a motherly fashion removed the wet sweater from my shoulders.

She seemed resigned to the fact that sooner or later she would have to do something with me. I didn't know where I was or where I needed to go, but I did know that Dr. Eva was going to be extremely mad at me. Not only had I wandered away from the house, but I had left her door unlocked. Colette left me at the table with a bowl of bouillon that the waiter had brought me.

She went to another table where a goateed gentleman, wearing a beret was reading a book. He had just asked the waiter for a match to light his cigarette, then waved him off when the waiter asked for his order. He looked up with irritation as he sensed Colette's presence beside him. The irritation turned quickly to a smile as he saw her. He motioned to the empty chair next to his. With his other hand he signaled for the waiter to come back and immediately ordered two Pernods. At first Colette and he spoke seriously, then their conversation must have become amusing because their laughter became louder and louder.

I was drinking the last of my bouillon from the bowl when I looked up to see her leaving arm in arm with the strange man. I got up from my chair calling after her, *"Mademoiselle, mademoiselle."* She looked over her shoulder and told me to wait at the table and that she would return soon.

I thought of many things as I sat there. Apprehension welled up in me. It would soon be time for Dr. Eva to be back. She had told me to stay home and I had disobeyed her. What was I going to do? Even if Colette came back I knew that she wouldn't know what do with me. I knew the address of our house of course, but if everyone was trying to get me away from there, I probably should not go back right now. I had no idea why the Germans would want a six-year-old boy. I knew that I had not done anything that bad. I had heard that they were taking Jewish children my age away from their parents and throwing them on trucks. We were Catholic, so how could all this be?

I looked toward the door; Colette was returning by herself. Just as she reached the door, a German officer took her arm and pulled her back out onto the sidewalk. I must have looked scared because the waiter came to the table and stood looking at me with his back to the door obstructing my view and at the same time, that of someone standing outside.

Colette and the German officer spoke for awhile, then she left with him. I thought that she certainly was a friendly person, but mostly to adults.

The waiter walked away from my table as I looked out of the window just in time to see Dr. Eva walking hurriedly by. I jumped up and ran out after her. I caught up to her and pulled at her arm. She glanced down in disbelief. "Let's hurry home, we will talk there, I have a lot to tell you" she said. She did not even seem angry that I had disobeyed her. She took my hand and walked so fast that I had to trot to keep up with her. The rain had stopped, but the cold reminded me of her sweater. I told her that we had to go back, her sweater was there drying. She told me no! She would get it another time and for me to hurry. I stumbled a few times trying to keep up. My head was swimming with the day's events.

Chapter Three

Dr. Eva opened the unlocked the door to her apartment, yanked me in by the shoulder, then slammed the door behind me. She unwrapped her scarf and dropped a valise on a chair. I knew that I was in trouble, but I also recognized the valise that my father had given me for our vacation trips to *Ile de Ré*. I remembered the discussion he and I had when he stuck the decal of the Hotel Palatinus in Budapest on top of it. Seriously, he had said that some day that hotel would be mine.

I looked up from the valise to see Dr. Eva, hands on hips, glaring at me through moist eyes. She looked at me without saying anything for what seemed an eternity. Then gently she reached down, took my hand and drew me to the bed. She told me that she had seen my mother who had sent me my clothes. I asked why Maman had not come to get me to take me home. Dr. Eva seemed to hesitate then she simply said that she had not been able to today. Then I asked where my father was. She said that he had gone away but my mother had found out where he was. She had not been able to see him but had received a note from him and had written him back but she felt sure that he would not return for a few weeks. "No more questions now, we have to get you ready for your trip, your mother has arranged for you to go visit your grandparents on *Ile de Ré*."

Dr. Eva put two large pots of water on her stove to heat. When they came to a boil she emptied them in the bathtub, drew two more and brought them to a boil. As she added water from the tap she told me to get undressed for my bath. She asked if I usually bathed alone? I told her that sometimes my father would wash my back. I was amazed that she had used that much gas to heat water for my bath. She finished adjusting the temperature and told me to get in.

I played with a sponge, washing my left arm, when I looked up. She had taken her clothes off and was stepping into the tub behind me. She told me not to turn around and said that she could wash my back better this way and anyway she wanted to take a bath too. She explained that if she waited until I was finished the water would be cold. My head snapped around looking forward at my feet. She took my sponge, applied a soap that smelled like my grandmother's lilac tree and gently rubbed my back and under my arms. She said, "Do you want to wash my back?" I don't remember if I was old enough to blush but I do remember shaking my head, no. She laughed throatily and ruffled my hair. She soaped it and then dunked me to rinse it.

She told me that if I was not going to wash her back I should get out and let her bathe. I was drying myself as I hurried into the cold room to find some clean underwear from my valise. I sat on the bed not sure what to do next. Usually I went to bed immediately after my bath, on the nights I had a bath, but today it was only five o'clock.

Dr. Eva ran out of the bathroom wrapped in a towel jumped into her bed and threw the towel to the floor. She lifted the corner of the covers, smiled and said "come in, we need to warm you up". I hesitated but I was really cold so I eased into the bed and turned my back to her. She reached for me and turned me over by the shoulders and pulled me toward her. At first I stiffened but she said, "it's all right". I let her pull my head against her naked breasts and she held me tight for a few minutes. She sobbed gently as her tears flowed onto my forehead. I looked up to ask her why she was crying but she gently pushed my face back between her breasts and squeezed me again. I let myself follow the contour of her body until I realized where I was, then I froze. She laughed through the tears, kissed the top of my head and said "Someday, you will remember this afternoon, then you'll wish you had been older."

We lay there for what seemed a long time but in reality could not have been more than a half-hour. Dr. Eva pushed back the covers, swung her legs off the bed, sat up and walked away in one fluid motion. This time I looked. She had such a small waist and a wide bottom, almost like one of the paintings I had seen in the Louvre. She looked in the mirror and our eyes met. She said seriously, "Don't ever forget me or how I look". I swore that I would not.

She dressed all in black, except for a red and white polka dot silk scarf that she knotted around her neck. I thought that my father must have given it to her since he always wore blue and white polka dot neckties. She took some green shorts that resembled "lederhosen" and a shirt out of my valise. In those days French boys didn't wear "lederhosen", they had belonged to Serge. Dr. Eva helped me dress, then we sat back on the bed. She put her arms around me again and said in a low voice "You have to go on a trip by yourself. You are a little man and I know that you will be all right." A wave of fear came over me. Where was I going? She sounded so serious, as if she would never see me again. "A lady was to take you to La Palice but she is unable to go. You will take the train to La Rochelle, then you will go to your grandparents' house. Now you must listen very carefully. I will take you to the train at the Gare Montparnasse. Here is an envelope you must give to the conductor when he comes in your compartment to collect the tickets. A lady will meet you in La Rochelle. Go with her to her house. Tomorrow she will take you to the Captain of the ferryboat from La Palice to Sablanceaux. He will pretend that you are his sister's son. There you will meet your *grandpere*".

I was fascinated by what she was saying. I had made this trip several times with my parents but she wanted me to take a trip half way across France by myself. As a form of reassurance she told me that this would help make a strong man out of me.

It was almost dark and we had a long way to go. She reached for her raincoat with the yellow star on it. From the pocket she pulled out a police whistle and a toy pistol that shot matches. She gave them both to me and told me to be sure not to blow the whistle if there were any Germans around.

Dr. Eva took a final look around her apartment, picked up my valise and put my school satchel around my neck, then pushed me out into the street. We headed for the "Metro" that would take us to the "Gare Montparnasse." I pulled out my whistle and blew it a couple of times to make sure that it worked. As patient as Dr. Eva was she lost her composure. She yanked the whistle out of my hand, put it back in my pocket, almost yelling at me to keep it there at night.

Journey Two

Paris to Ile de Ré

Chapter Four

I was in a cold and damp compartment all by myself, on top of that I was hungry and tired. Dr. Eva placed my valise on the overhead rack, gave me the usual three kisses on the cheeks and left hurriedly.

The train station was full of new sounds. The hiss of venting steam and the sound of engines straining to get under way were enticing to a small boy. I stuck my head out of the open window, through the two horizontal safety bars. The train lurched ahead, so I pulled my head back to return to my seat but nothing happened. I pulled and pulled, to no avail. One bar was under my chin and the other on the back of my head. The train reached cruising speed as another train came into the station on the adjacent track, seeming to just miss my head.

I panicked, there was still no one else in the compartment and I knew I couldn't stay like that. The conductor slid the door open, while shouting at me to close that window. We were supposed to be under blackout to keep the bombers from seeing the train. I still couldn't move, and all the yelling was not helping. Finally, he realized my predicament and broke into a deep uproarious laugh. *"Alors mon vieux, tu a perdue ta tete."* Well I had not lost my head yet but it seemed that I would. In spite of his gruffness he reached around my head and with practiced hands, turned it sideways and gently eased it back. He slammed the window closed and pulled down the shade.

He asked where my mother was? He didn't say parents, probably because very few men were still traveling as civilians. I remembered that I was to give him the envelope that Dr. Eva had placed in my satchel. I rummaged around in my school satchel until I found it, then handed it to the conductor without a word. He started reading, I heard him say *"merde"* under his breath as he pushed the visored *kepi* back on his head. He turned slightly, as if to hide the fact that he was pocketing the bills. I was always very observant and saw the money going into the breast pocket of his uniform.

He asked for my identification card. I didn't have one. He said, "Any child traveling alone was to have identification!" Well, I didn't have any, so what was I to do? He looked at me, shook his head, took my valise off the rack and told me to come with him. We walked through two swaying cars into first class. He looked around and quickly opened the door into a roomette. He pushed me in, pulled the top berth down and lifted me into it. He told me to stay there until he came back to get me. He walked out and locked the door behind him.

The door opening woke me. I sensed that the train had stopped. The next thing I knew the conductor was standing next to me telling me not to be afraid. He helped me down then stuffed me under the bottom bunk. It reminded me of my large wood and wicker toy box. I often climbed in and closed the lid, opening the door to my make believe world. I could then become the hero of one of my father's bedtime tales. Once, I even spent the afternoon sleeping in the belly of a whale. Anyway, the darkness and the closeness didn't bother me; but I really had to go to the bathroom.

I heard sharp voices for a brief moment; then the door closed and all was quiet. After what seemed an eternity, the train resumed its journey south; the conductor pulled me out and replaced me on the top bunk. In passing he mentioned that he had a son just about my age.

The rest of the trip was uneventful and I slept. The conductor woke me again. This time he was accompanied by a lady wearing a dirty, white woolen scarf. She grabbed my shoulder and jerked me to my feet. She was very brusque and almost dragged me behind her.

I had become accustomed to the kindness of strangers during the previous few days, this lady's manner took me back a little, she was not hurting me; she only seemed to be in a hurry. The conductor followed closely behind us. My new custodian stepped off the train, and as the conductor helped me down the steps, she was already walking briskly away. It was not quite daylight yet; a small yellow light in the distance seemed to beckon to us; but with little confidence or welcome. Nevertheless, we headed toward it. We hurried past the small stone shack at the side of the station. Through the broken windowpanes, I saw the silhouette of a man huddled over an oil lamp, intent on warming his hands by the glass chimney.

We continued across two sets of tracks, onto a cobbled street. Several blocks away, we turned and suddenly went down three or four worn stone steps, below street level. My escort closed the door behind us; immediately a wave of dampness came over me. We walked around unrecognizable objects piled on the floor, and climbed another set of stone steps to a door that opened into a badly lit room. It reeked of perspiration, stale tobacco and wet wool. A coal fired stove was the only source of heat.

The lady didn't seem quite as brusque in the house, but she was still very distant. She pointed to a cot in the corner furthest from the stove and told me to lie down. She said she would come wake me at daylight. She bolted the stairway door and left the room.

I lay there pondering my last adventure, wondering what was to come next?

It seemed that I had just gone to sleep when a severe shaking woke me. A man dressed in denim, wearing a fisherman's hat, looked down at me through the smoke of the cigarette hanging from the corner of his mouth. I remember his " *Eh! mon gros, vien*". ("Well my big one, come!"). I rubbed my eyes, hesitating to go with this stranger. But I rationalized that for the last week I had been only with strangers, and I was still fine. So I got up, still dressed from the previous day.

We went into an unheated small room, an alcove, curtained from the kitchen/living room. We sat at a small round table covered with blue and white checkered oilcloth. It was set with two bowls and a spoon for each. One of the folding leaves was down against the wall. The fisherman handed me the heel of old bread, and took one for himself, breaking it up in bite size pieces. He went back to the stove, I heard him exclaim "*merde*", (it seemed that everyone used that word; my father had told me to never say it) and as he came back with a pot of milk, I saw the side where the milk had boiled over and burned. He poured the milk over the bread and we both ate as if we were starving. I thought about it and realized that a day and a half had passed, since I had eaten.

I ate and thought; soon I would be with my Mamie and Pepére. I had a room upstairs in their house that I generally shared with Serge. Since he was at the *lycée*, I would have it all to myself.

The fisherman finished his, told me to hurry, as he rolled a cigarette, dipping his "Zig Zag" paper, into an oilskin tobacco pouch. I was puzzled. Why rush? Since I was supposed to take the ferry later that day. So I asked him. He told me there was no ferry this week. The bombs had sunk a ship right in the channel, so he decided to take me across in his fishing boat. There was a *charrette*, a two-wheeled cart that looked like a small version of a horse drawn cart, parked by the side door. It was loaded with wicker baskets used to store the fish catch.

I still had my book sack around my neck, but my valise was no where in sight. I asked my captain about my valise. He knew nothing of a valise and said he didn't think that I had one. I insisted that I had a valise, and that I needed it. My insistence got me a slap in the face for insolence, then a boost into one of the fish baskets. He inverted another basket over me, and told me to be quiet. I was still objecting about my valise, but I wasn't going to cry because of the slap.

He picked up the arms of the *charrette*, placed a rope harness over his shoulders, and started pushing. The iron rimmed, wooden wheel, rolling on the cobbled streets had my teeth chattering. It seemed like a half-hour later, when we finally stopped on the quay of the harbor.

I looked through the weave of my basket. I could see fishing boats heeled over, resting on the muddy bottom of the harbor. I had often seen such low tides in La Flotte, during my many walks to the harbor with Pepére.

The muddy harbor bottom, was etched randomly, with shallow channels; allowing a small amount of dinghy traffic. Boys, destined to be fishermen, as their ancestors had been for generations before them, sculled the family dinghies, bringing provisions in preparation of the day's sailing. Meager as they were, rations for each boat consisted of bread, lard, and unbleached flour; the necessities for frying fresh fish at sea. A couple bottles of the captain's wine, topped off the fare. Each seaman brought his own beverage. Again, I looked around through my range of vision, but didn't see a boat that I thought we would board.

I lifted the top basket from my niche, to start getting up. My fisherman quickly pushed me down, and replaced the cover. He told me to stay, until I was told that it was all right for me to move.

My legs were beginning to cramp, so I called "*Monsieur, M'sieur, M'sieur*!" There was no answer. I turned around in my basket and a few meters away, I saw him talking with a group of fishermen. They were all turned facing my *charrette*. I couldn't hear what was said but the expressions on their faces told me that they were not very happy.

A long time passed; then I saw the boats start to right themselves on the inrushing tide. I looked back at the group just as a German soldier walked up holding out his hands. His autoritative voice demanded "*papiers*!" My heart pounded as they reached in their pockets and pulled out the necessary identification cards. He made quite a production of mounting his monocle on his right eye. He studied each card thoroughly, then leaned forward matching the individual with the photograph on his card. This done, he seemed to become more pleasant and told them in his heavily accented French, to have "*une bonne peche*".

My fisherman waited until the German had left his group and moved on to another, to walk back to my *charrette*. Without a word he picked the fork and started rolling me toward a slanted, loading area in the quay. Once there, he brought the *charrette* as close to the waiting boat as possible. He swung the baskets to one of the crew on board. The crewman in turn dropped them down to another deck hand in the hold. When he reached mine, the captain said in a low voice "*attention*!" My baskets were slid on the deck, instead of going in the hold.

The captain anxious to leave, grasped the engine flywheel by the handle and rapidly cranked it to start the one cylinder diesel. The two crewmembers cast off the lines as he started backing away from the quay. He was far enough out to clear the boat ahead of us, when he shifted into forward gear. The boat eased ahead, went fifteen or twenty meters, then plunged bow down and shuddered to a stop, sending almost everything on deck forward.

We were the first boat to cast off. We were also the first boat to get stuck in the mud. My captain didn't get much pity from his fellow sailors. They called out to him in good humor, but there was no offer of help. This was the beginning of my realization that you are responsible for your actions. In spite of occasional outside help, ultimately you have to take care of yourself. We waited "amud", until the tide came in sufficiently for us to break loose from the suction that held the boat. Strangely, I never saw nor heard the name of the boat.

We cleared the harbor towers that were built under orders of Cardinal Richelieu in the mid-sixteen twenties. They were to close off the harbor by connecting boats with huge chains and floating them from tower to tower.

The deck hands set the two faded brown sails, patched through the years with orange and yellow remnants of older sails. We motored well out of sight of the harbor, the hands slid my basket forward to the wheelhouse, and as the sails began to draw, the captain killed the engine. He lifted the top basket and told me to get inside the wheelhouse. I stood up to go in, and promptly fell to my knees. My legs were so numb that I couldn't stand. I crawled inside on hands and knees, my book satchel still around my neck. I was not letting that go at any cost.

The trip was uneventful. We headed out in the

Straits of Antioche for what seemed an eternity, but in reality were probably only a couple of hours. The boats that had sailed before us seemed to go in different directions. Each captain had his favorite fishing ground. The deck hands prepared the net for launching. The floats were glass balls and doughnut shaped corks. The weather was good, though the sky stayed gray all day. The boat rocked and pitched constantly. I was a bit woozy, but not really ill. The captain broke off a piece of bread and handed it to me to settle my stomach. I climbed up on a built in bench, then went to sleep.

I awoke, late in the afternoon, to the sound of squeaking gears. A rusty, hand driven windlass was used to pull in the nets. Evidently they had been brought in several times before; the hampers on deck were half full of assorted types of fish.

We fished all day. Toward dusk, the nets were brought in for the last time. I looked forward, realizing that we were moving slowly in the direction of land, visible in the distance. The deck hands were finishing their tasks, readying the boat for docking. One of the sailors had his hand through a loop in a hemp rope, connected to the bail of the wooden bucket. He dropped it overboard several times, bringing up water to scrub the deck. On one throw, the weight of the bucket and the motion of the boat, almost pulled him over. He cursed a few times and rubbed his wrist.

For the better part of the trip no one spoke to me or even acknowledged that I was there. Their work done, they came into the cabin and started talking about the day's catch and the next day's weather.

The captain gave the wheel to one of the hands, walked outside and looked at the fish, some in the hampers, others in wooden crates with the rope handles. He came back, reached in his knapsack, and pulled out a liter of *gros rouge,* took a big swallow and passed the bottle around. One of the crew handed it to me, I shook my head "no" and they all laughed. They tried to convince me to have some, but I held firm.

I looked at the horizon and could barely make out the land ahead. I asked if that was where we were going, and how long it would take to get there? The camaraderie, after good day's catch, seemed to relax everyone. The Captain told me, "Yes; and we would arrive before dark."

Eventually, we pulled into the back part of the small harbor of Sablanceaux on *Ile de Ré*. They tied up the boat. The captain jumped on shore and turned toward one of the crew, who handed me across to him.

We walked to another cold house, a few meters from where the boat was tied up. I was guided into a back room. Immediately after, I heard a heated discussion, through the partially closed door. "*Le gosse*", came up several times again. People always seemed to get mad when they talked about me.

I sat on a cane chair and waited for what was to come next. I was awake enough for my mind to start working again. Why did these people take my valise? I didn't know them but they had helped me. Surely they must be helping me for money too, like the train conductor. Then I realized that I didn't remember getting the valise off the train. The lady had been in such a hurry that she didn't even know about it. The conductor must have ended up with it, probably hoping that my clothes would fit his son.

I was now on *Ile de Ré* where Pepére and Mamie lived. They were in La Flotte seven kilometers away. I didn't know how to get there from where I was, but I was sure that I could find them. I thought of sneaking out of a window, and just setting out on the road. I had waited too long!

The door opened. The faint yellowish light of a single bulb outlined the figure of a squat, elderly woman, as she shuffled into the room.

She placed her open hand on my forehead as if to check me for a fever. I was surprised by the gentleness of her voice when she told me that I would stay there until morning. The light from the open door enabled me to see a settee against the far wall. She told me to go lie down; she would wake me when it was time. My hostess helped me up on the settee, took off my shoes, and covered me with a huge feather comforter. Surprisingly, she kissed me on the forehead. I was asleep in less than a minute.

I awoke with a start. At first I had no idea where I was or what woke me. Then I heard muffled voices, behind the partially opened door. I didn't know whether to get up or stay in bed. Curiosity getting the better of me, I emerged from under the feather bed and hesitantly opened the squeaking door. The conversation stopped. My hostess half smiled, and recognizing my needs, took me outside, and showed me the "outhouse".

I had never seen one quite like that. It must have been for the entire family. There was a high bench with two openings, one larger than the other, and on the left there was a lower seat for children. Each opening had covers with leather straps for hinges. Perfectly cut squares of old newspaper hung on a nail behind each seat. My business completed, I went back inside. I didn't know the lady's name and she was not inclined to tell me what it was. She asked if I knew the way to my grandparent's house from the harbor in La Flotte? I replied, "Yes I did!"

We left the house and walked several hundred meters to railroad tracks. Instead of a train there was a *Micheline*, (a bus converted to travel on railroad tracks) empty with the door closed. We waited, seated on a backless wooden bench. Finally a man smoking a pipe, looking more like a fisherman than a train engineer, limped to the door of the "*Micheline*" opened it and climbed in. He leaned down and called around his pipe, "*Allons nous*!" The half-hour ride to *La Flotte* was punctuated at each joint of the tracks, with a monotonous, metallic click clack.

I was let out where the tracks curved above the town, but that was not near the harbor. I set out down the small hill that did take me to the "*Rue du Port*." I walked down past the *Boulangerie* with the smell of fresh bread, then further past *Monsieur Claudomire's Charcuterie.* I turned left up the *Ruelle* and after several turns I came to the back door of the house I knew well. I knocked on the door. Pepére opened it, looked down at me and asked what I wanted; and as an afterthought, if I was lost? I thought, surely, he must not be serious. He was squinting at me through his usually dirty, metal rimmed glasses. I told him who I was. He rushed me in, called "Lucie!" in a shaky voice. Mamie came swinging her arthritic legs from the hips, dropped her two canes as she plopped in a kitchen chair, wrapped her arms around me and started crying.

Pepére said that he had tried to meet me at the train stop, but couldn't leave the house. Word had come down from the island German command by the town crier that, "All French men were to stay off the streets and roads that morning". The Germans were holding maneuvers.

The next few weeks were uneventful. I had the three rooms upstairs to explore by myself. Mamie had not been able to climb stairs in years. My parent's room had a beautiful desk, with a secret compartment. Pepére gave me an old alarm clock that hadn't worked in ages. I was able to disassemble it and then put it back together. One day it even worked for a few hours. There was a high closet above the clothes closet, full of Pepére's old toys. I pulled a small table up and hoisted a chair onto it. Standing on my toes I was able to pull out a small accordion that intrigued me. I played with it for days, and even learned to play a bit of "*Au claire de la lune*" on it. There was also a book with color pictures of fruit. I took it downstairs to ask Pepére what some of the ones I had never seen were. He told me about oranges, bananas and grapefruit. He also said, "Someday, you will see them again and be able to taste their goodness".

The village priest had arranged with my grandmother and the Mother Superior, for me to attend the Catholic school nearby. Since it was only a few blocks away, I could walk there using back streets to stay out of sight. Later, when the Germans were accustomed to seeing me, I was to enroll in the public school.

As far as I remember, I did well in school. I was only punished once. I'm afraid that my transgression (it had something to do with multiplication tables) has long since been forgotten. The penalty has not! It entailed extending my hands, palms up, bringing my fingers and thumb together to a point, and enduring my sentence of blows to the tips of my fingers from the square ruler. The penalty for dropping ones hands called for doubling the number of blows.

Christmas was a blur. I went to midnight mass with neighbors, Suzanne and her mother. Pepére claimed to be a descendant of the Huguenots from when they occupied *Ile de Ré*. His friends joked that he had used that excuse for years, to keep from going to church; any church. I had made Christmas cards for each of them that I presented proudly in the morning. Otherwise, there was no commemoration of the day. No gifts were exchanged; there was really nothing in the stores to buy on the island.

A couple of weeks prior to Christmas, Pepére had

received a letter telling him to be at the post office at a specified time, to answer a telephone call. The post office was the site of the only public telephone in town.

Mamie and I knew of his appointment, but nothing else. He left in plenty of time to receive the call. When he returned, I was sent to my room. My curiosity as keen as ever, prompted me to quietly sneak down the stairs, within hearing of the kitchen. Pepére was recounting the telephone conversation to Mamie.

I understood that my mother had called, explaining my father's disappearance. The "Gestapo" had taken my father. He had been part of a group of people helping Jews escape from France. He had been transferred from one jail to another. She was really afraid. People from the new jail were generally sent east, probably to Poland. She had been unable to find out anything else. The Gestapo, accompanied by the French police, had returned to our house with questions about my papers and me. It seemed that my baptismal certificate had been altered and they still wanted to see my birth certificate. Maman told them that I was away for my health and that I would be returning soon. They told her to be sure to contact the police when I returned to Paris. She agreed and that seemed to satisfy them for the moment.

Pepére told Mamie that I was to be evacuated into hiding as soon as possible. A group was working on finding me a place to live, on a farm, somewhere in central France. Serge was all right, since he had a different last name. He would stay in a new school in "Thouars".

Chapter Five

It was not a simple matter to find a farm family who would take the chance of boarding me. My mother wanted me hidden, but she wanted it to be done with some type of comfort. She was told that she was too particular. She should simply send me to a colony with other children my age, I would be lost among the others. She had a pretty good network of informers through her office that kept her apprised of any change in status. She felt that I was still pretty safe in La Flotte, at least as long as I didn't get in a situation having to have to show some types of identification. She decided that I would stay with Pepére and Mamie a little longer.

During the month of May, I became ill with a very high fever. The nearest doctor was in *St. Martin*, several kilometers away. Due to fuel shortage and the large number of patients, he could only come to La Flotte three days a month. He had practiced medicine for many years but his expertise was in farm injuries, delivering babies and attempting to cure colds. He came to see me three times, each time injecting me with solutions of camphor and eucalyptus. This had very little success. Mamie was an invalid and had been unable to climb stairs for over ten years. A bed had been moved to the living room for her use. I was placed in her bed while she slept in a chair. It was impossible for her to care for me by herself. Some of the neighbors came in during the day to help.

I was subjected to a number of "cures". One was the traditional mustard plaster, chest and back. Another was the "*vantouse*", I believe they were called "cupping glasses". This semi barbaric process required dropping an ignited alchohol soaked cotton ball into the jar. This vessel was then quickly inverted allowing the burning cotton to evacuate the air causing a partial vacuum. The skin and soft tissue was sucked into the jar allowing the extraction of infection through the pores. The process was repeated until the entire back was covered with jars. I am certain that there were other "remedies" but I don't remember them.

The Doctor reached the extent of his ability after the third week. The word to the family was that he had done all he could. "The rest was up to God, but, there was little hope." He didn't come back even though I was in and out of consciousness. The entire village had heard of his surrender. The residents were upset that the doctor was unable to save this child's life.

I was told that three days after the Doctor's pronouncement Pepére saw a German staff car drive up to his house. There was a knock on the seldom-used front door. Friends and family used the back door that opened into the kitchen. Mamie panicked, fearing for my safety. She thought that surely they would not take me when I was so sick.

Pepere limped to the door, his hip had been fractured during a bicycle fall a few years before. He threw the door open thinking that such a bold move might confuse the person knocking. A German officer, speaking fluent French, introduced himself as a doctor who had heard that a young boy was dying in this village. He said that he didn't know what he could do, but he would at least like to examine him.

He looked at me and said " He is nothing but eyes and bones". He asked where my mother was, Pepere hesitated to tell him. The Doctor told him not to be concerned, and that "Yes! He was German, but above all he was a Doctor, and a dying child should have his mother with him." Dr. Metzger ordered his chauffeur to send a telegram to her address using the police in Paris to prepare a pass for her. She would have to pick it up, then have it countersigned at the German headquarters not far from her office.

Later that evening in Paris, my mother answered the doorbell recoiling in fear. One of the two policemen standing there handed her the telegram that they had evidently read. They were not only apologetic for disturbing her, but were also sympathetic as they handed her the message. They told her exactly how to obtain the pass, with the least amount of problems, this even before she had read the contents.

The instant they left, she reread the words through tearful eyes. This was such a shock! She had been under the impression that all was well with us, then she received a telegram telling her that I was dying. She had to wait until the offices opened the next morning to obtain the pass. She tried to sleep to rest for the trip, but she couldn't. She stayed awake all night, packing and unpacking a small valise. Anything to pass the time.

Early the next morning she set out to obtain her pass, following the instructions of the two policemen. A French employee of the Germans held out the already prepared pass without any problem. She had to get it countersigned and that took hours. Fortunately, the regular police had not attached any significance to our name. Only the Gestapo was interested in my whereabouts.

Maman had taken a small valise with her so she could go directly to the Gare Montparnasse. The train was ready for departure, but she was told that German soldiers had taken all the seats, so she would have to wait for another train leaving the next morning. She ran back to the stationmaster's office and showed him the pass and the telegram saying that said I was dying. He gave her a ticket but told her that it only allowed her to stand for the entire trip. She was exhausted physically and mentally. She hoped that there would be a gentleman among the German soldiers who might offer his seat, even for an hour. She stood all night, except for a short time that she sat on the cold floor.

Providence on her side, the ferry to the island was running. She arrived in Sablanceaux only to find that the *micheline* was out of order. She walked and ran the seven kilometers to La Flotte, in the heat of the June morning. She arrived at the house, shoes under her arm, valise in one hand, and suit jacket dragging the ground from the other. Dr. Metzger had arrived just moments before her to check on me. She ran into my room, dropping everything on the floor, by the back door. The doctor saw that she was exhausted and quickly sent her to bed with a warning that she also would get sick, if she didn't rest. He told her not to worry that he would care for me and save me.

Soon, I started improving, and Dr. Metzger only came once a day, then every other day. One pleasant morning I was able to go outside to Pepére's garden, the one that was just two hundred meters away. I was too weak to walk, so maman carried me like a babe in arms, protecting me from even the slightest breeze. Still, that night my fever went back up and my ears started hurting.

Maman sent word to Dr. Metzger. He did come in the morning, but he was all packed to go on furlough. He was going to see his wife and two boys at his home in

Cologne. My mother understood his desire, since he had not seen his family for almost two years, but she was frantic. The weeks it had taken for me to improve went for nothing. The Doctor told her to have faith in him; he would make arrangements for a French surgeon and nurses to care for me in the hospital in La Rochelle. He reassured her that he would not leave until all the arrangements were confirmed; then he would return in two weeks to check on me.

Later an ambulance came with a nurse to pick me up. I was scheduled to have surgery early the next day. We went across on the ferry to La Rochelle.

Whether it was through my mother's prayers or the good care of the nurses, my abscessed ear ruptured by itself and surgery was not necessary. We stayed in the clinic two weeks. There was nothing there to amuse me, and there were no books to read for either of us. Maman had knitting needles and wool so she taught me to knit squares to make blankets for the French army hospitals.

The shrill wail of air raid sirens, followed quickly by the sound of exploding bombs, woke us almost nightly. The claxons of the fire trucks followed, racing, to reach survivors before the buildings crumbled not far from us. Still weak, and not completely well, I was given my release from the clinic, so we went back to La Flotte.

Serge's school term was finished, he was to meet us for his summer vacation, and the three of us would spend the time on the island with my grandparents.

Occasionally, bombs fell on the island, though the targets were generally ships anchored between La Rochelle and *Ile de Ré*. A few days later Serge arrived on the island. He was a mess! Dirty clothes and no luggage. We knew that everything he did was dramatic, (the artist in him) but even for him, that was a bit much.

He explained that he had escaped a bombing with his life. He had just boarded the ferry in La Palice when an air raid struck. He and the other passengers were ordered off the ferry, and told to find a safe place to hide. He was too far back to make it to the terminal as many had, before bombs began dropping all around. He jumped into an old crater, hoping that two bombs would never land in the same place. Seconds after he jumped into the crater a bomb struck and demolished the terminal taking many lives. A hotel and several houses close to the harbor also fell to this air raid.

The ferryboat would not run that day, so he spent the night in the crater, under a sheet of metal that he scavenged. The next day, the boat resumed service, so he boarded and came on to Ré. The *Micheline* again, was not running, so he set out on foot to La Flotte. A German truck going his way, slowed down long enough for him to jump on and ride to town.

His story told, he sat at the piano and played, while his bath water was warming on the coal fired stove. The three of us had now escaped death by bombs by just a few meters. What did it all mean? Mamie said it was divine providence, and there was to be a greater purpose to our lives. We should both go to the priest and ask for the meaning of all this. Undoubtedly, he would say that we should both prepare for the priesthood.

The next day Serge wanted to know about my father and what was to happen to the family.

Mother recapped the past few months since my father's imprisonment. The last time she and Serge had been together, was at Christmas in Paris. They had hoped to visit my father. The authorities told them that visits were allowed only after the prisoner had been incarcerated six months. Though it seemed like a year to her, my father had been in Compiegne slightly over two months. They were allowed to send a food parcel with a smoked sausage and a jar of jam.

Their Christmas meal consisted of the usual rutabaga with a small piece of bread and jam for desert. They exchanged gifts, maman gave Serge a piece of sheet music, and he had found her a small potted cactus. Christmas over, he had gone back to school and Maman had returned to her office job.

Late on the tenth of February she received a card from my father. He asked her to use any contact she had or that she might have known in the past to try to get an appeal. He was scheduled to go EAST, on the morning of the eleventh. She knew that East meant a concentration camp with hard labor or gas chambers. In any case the chances of his return were almost nonexistent.

From the time she received word, and late into the night, she telephoned French officials who might be favorable to her cause. She was unable to go see anyone in person since any citizen caught on the street after the curfew of nine o'clock would be arrested. The last telephone call she made was to a German official who had come to her office a few days before. Almost as if they all had rehearsed it, he said relatively the same thing that the French officials had said. Since she had tried for three months to have him released unsuccessfully, why did she think that she would succeed in a few hours? There would be no change in his situation, therefore she must simply accept his sentence.

Maman, devastated, made the decision to go to the prison early in the morning. She felt that if she could only speak to the commandant of the prison in German, she would certainly convince him to at least delay my father's trip east.

At four o'clock, the morning of February 11th, 1943 she took the chance of violating the curfew, and walked to the train station. Fortunately, there had been no air raid that night and the trains were running. She walked down dark unfamiliar streets, following the obscure instructions she had received from a man on the train, and arrived at the prison gate of Drancy, before daylight. The instant she arrived at the gate, a floodlight came on blinding her momentarily. She regained her vision, and saw both French gendarmes and German soldiers as sentinels in the wooden black and white striped gatehouses.

Full of bravado, she told the gendarme that she must speak to the German Commandant of the prison, and asked him to escort her to his quarters. The guards refused to let her pass telling her sadistically, that the buses were loaded with men, women and children prisoners, who were due to be sent to Germany or Poland. They would then be assigned to labor camps or concentration camps. Since the buses were ready to depart any minute, heading for the train station; she would have to leave.

She obeyed stepping back, but she would wait to see the buses, hoping to catch a glimpse of my father or at least to let him see that she was here with him. He had once written in an earlier letter that had reached her; "*I would give one year of my life if I could see you just one minute*".

Almost immediately she heard the sound of engines. The first bus paused at the huge iron gates, before turning into the street. She strained her eyes as she looked into the bus. She was certain that she saw a man reach up and touch his cap, the same kind she had sent my father earlier in a package of winter clothing. She knew that making any signs on his part was forbidden; usually under penalty of being shot.

The bus disappeared in the gloomy dawn; not even the hooded taillights were visible. She lost track of the count after thirty busses passed through the gate, then she started walking along behind them. It seemed that she walked for hours before she reached the "Station Le Bourget". She was not allowed to come into the station during the loading of the prisoners onto freight cars. She pleaded, fought and tried to bribe but all to no avail. Frustration triggered tears of helplessness and anger as she realized that another chapter in her life was ending.

Her vision occluded with tears, suffering from frustration and now hunger, maman returned home without knowing how she had done it.

Maman had left the apartment in the care of three Jewish ladies. Flora, her mother Eva and a lady whose name I don't remember. They had also lost their husbands in a roundup of Jews. Fortunately for them, they had been away from home together, and had been warned not to return to their apartments. They telephoned my mother, asking for refuge for a short time, they knew that she was Catholic and that my father had previously been arrested. They reasoned that perhaps her apartment would be safe. It was a good arrangement, they hid in the apartment for two years, and it was cared for. Maman did have to pay the concierge an outrageous amount of money, to keep her from reporting the ladies.

This story told; we were all brought up to date.

A week or so later, a letter from Flora came for maman, telling her that a man had telephoned several times looking for her. He would not give his name, but he did leave a telephone number. He had been with my father, and had something to give her.

It was almost impossible to obtain a pass to leave the island. Maman made up her mind that she would leave without one. She waited a few days when out of nowhere an opportunity arose. She convinced the driver of a furniture van, to let her hide in an *armoire* long enough to cross on the ferry, to the mainland. He agreed reluctantly, telling her that he was taking a terrible chance. If for some reason the guards suspected him, and looked in the furniture, they could both be shot. She would not be able to take a valise. She placed her toilet articles and a few necessities in a small shoe bag.

Anyone who moved around, away from home, was accustomed to taking chances; and survived by instinct. They cleared through the checkpoint, after a soldier's half hearted look into the truck. The guard post was manned by middle aged soldiers, who really didn't want to be there, anymore than the islanders wanted them there. They didn't consider themselves Nazis; they were just good Germans and obeying orders. The trip for her was not comfortable, but it was uneventful.

Two weeks later she returned. I'm not sure how. She spoke of her trip but said nothing of my father. Finally, with a lump in my throat, I asked her for news about him. She waited an instant to answer, fighting back tears, then she said; "There was nothing new about him, but he must have known that he probably would never return. Before he boarded the bus, on the day I was there, he took off his ring and gave it and his silver razor to a fellow prisoner along with a penciled note and a short letter. *Monsieur Korda*, was to be released in a few weeks. He promised your father that he would deliver them only to me for you". She placed the ring in my hand and tenderly closed my fingers around it, showed me the razor that I knew so well, and took out the note. She started to read it. Tears welled up in her eyes. She turned her head, handed the note and the letter to Pepére and went upstairs to her room. Pepére read the letter hesitantly, as if not wishing to intrude on their privacy. Then he read the note.

February 10, 1943

My only love,
Tomorrow morning at daybreak we are leaving! Our destination is unknown, as is our fate. Still I hope to come back some day to embrace you and the children, to kiss the ones who kept some affection for me.
Can I tell you how I would have loved to see you even but once, if only for a minute? All is finished!
Live happy my beloved ones. You who were my love; Serge and Guy, who were my hope, stay united as much as possible.
Faithfulness that I asked of you in marriage keep it for our sons. Never let them go away from you while they need you.
Live your life. - I face an unknown future. - I go away with your radiant face in my heart.

G.

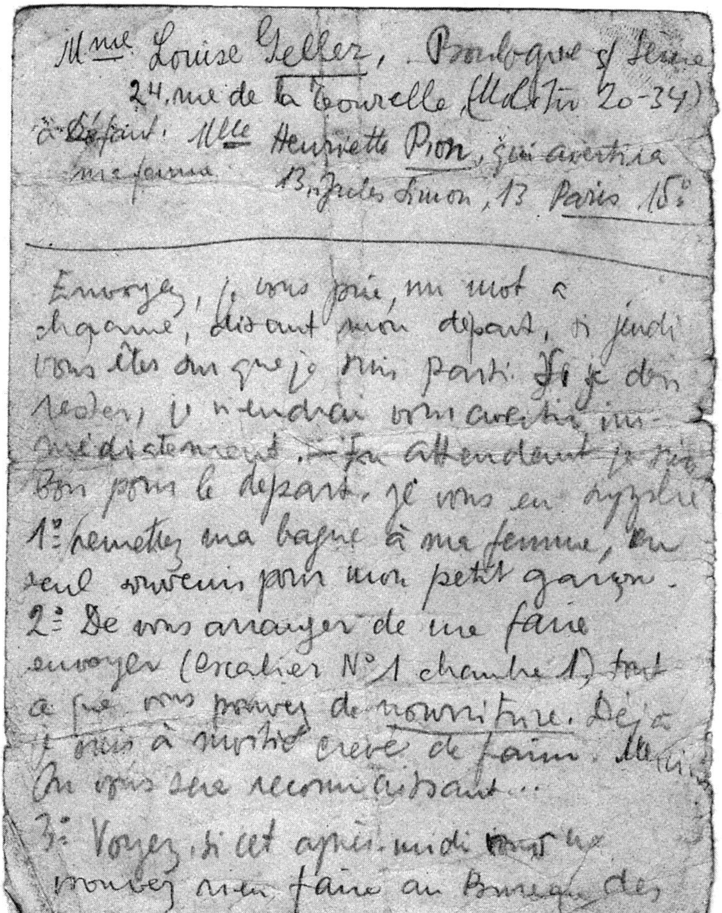

Mme Louise Geller, Boulogne s/ Seine
24, rue de la Tourelle (Molitor 20-34)
à défaut: Mlle Henriette Pion, qui avertira ma femme
13, r. Jules Simon, 13 Paris 15e

Envoyez, je vous prie, un mot à chacune, disant mon départ, si jeudi vous êtes sûr que je suis parti. Si je dois rester, je viendrai vous avertir immédiatement. ~~En attendant je suis~~ Bon pour le départ. Je vous en supplie
1° Remettez ma bague à ma femme, un seul souvenir pour mon petit garçon.
2° De vous arranger de me faire envoyer (Escalier N° 1 chambre 1) tout ce que vous pouvez de nourriture. Déjà je suis à moitié crevé de faim. Mais on vous sera reconnaissant...
3° Voyez si cet après-midi vous ne pouvez rien faire au Bureau des

Reproduction of original note.

Chapter Six

The next few weeks were pretty quiet. Serge had gone back to school in Thouars, a city much closer to us than Fontainebleau. Again this time a bombing raid close to his train had made the passengers jump out and hide under the freight cars; this was getting to be old stuff for him since every trip seemed to result in a near death experience. He would stay in school until vacation; that appeared to be safer.

Dr. Metzger came to see how I was doing. He asked my grandfather if he could take me for a ride? Pepére had been wounded by a German bullet in World War I and didn't like the Germans at all. He didn't trust, and was never very friendly toward the doctor, but somehow he agreed to let me go.

The doctor's driver headed north. I had never been to that end of the small island. We drove through several villages for my first time, arriving at the fortifications close to Ars. There, German soldiers were building, steel reinforced, concrete pillboxes, as part of a chain of battlements. We stepped out of the car and walked along a temporary road. The soldiers stopped digging and saluted.
Dr. Metzger told me to salute back, that the salutes were for me. I didn't understand what he meant. Even at my age I wouldn't give the Nazi salute so I pretended not to under-

stand his request. As kind and patient as he was I could tell that Dr. Metzger was angry that I would not raise my right arm to "Heil Hitler". He started walking faster until we got back in the car; he gave the driver instructions to go straight back to "11 Rue Gaston Lem".

A few weeks later the bombing intensified. The larger cities and the coastal towns were almost daily targets. The war had made all of us so callous. We could watch dogfights between British and German planes without attaching human life to them. We simply observed what seemed to be an aerial demonstration instead of mortal combat. The sky would fill with black puffs of smoke from the anti-aircraft batteries positioned on the mainland across from the island. Almost every encounter resulted in a hit by either side. Seconds after a strike, the plane erupted in flames and a cloud of black smoke. Then watching, the flaming, twisting dive, we wished for the sign of an opening parachute, before the unfortunate wreck plunged into the sea. On seeing the white canopy open, we could still utter a sigh of relief and give a silent cheer.

Once a downed English pilot landed not far from a field where one of Pepere's friends was working. Truckloads of German soldiers were dispatched to find him. By the time they arrived, he had already been hidden, and mysteriously, no one had seen him. Later, he was taken out to sea on a fishing boat, to rendezvous with supporters who would insure his return to England.

On the other hand, rumor had it, that when German pilots parachuted and were captured by the "underground", they were executed, and their bodies were dumped in a painter's quicklime pit to decompose. One of our neighbors, a house painter, had one of the concrete pits in his back courtyard. The mixture of quicklime and water bubbled constantly, but even more so, when the wooden stirrer with the burned end was used to agitate it. The real purpose of the pit, was to make whitewash for houses.

Pepére announced one day, that we needed a bomb shelter. The most practical place he decided, was in the garden closest to the house. It was large enough that if the perimeter walls caved in they would not fall on the shelter. There was always the slight chance of a direct hit, but he felt that he had chosen the right place.

The next morning we outlined a trench five or six meters long and about two meters wide, then started digging. The third or fourth day he hit some large stones. Using a pick, he managed to dislodge a couple, which dropped straight down into a hole. The pungent smell of sulfur escaping rushed at us from the hole. I recognized the odor, because Pepére used sulfur sticks to do away with gophers. He inverted his shovel and pushed the handle into the hole.

Pepére exited, felt certain that this was a part of the same tunnel he had discovered twenty years before. Then, he had found a large flat stone in the dirt floor of his shop, close to an outside wall. After digging down and around, he found another stone step that continued below ground level. He dug down as far as he was able, but just didn't have the strength to continue more than four or five meters. He found pots, pottery and even a ring.

History or legend had it that Benedictine monks had dug an escape tunnel from the eleventh century "*Abbey de St. Laurent-des-Chateliers*" between La Flotte and Rivedoux. Though it was nothing but ruins, having been demolished, then reconstructed in 1468 and later abandoned in 1623, Notre Dame de Ré, as it was then known, had always intrigued him.

This abandonment was in the same period as the construction of the towers in the harbor of La Rochelle. It was also during the time that the Huguenots under the leadership of Soubise seized both islands (then spelled Rhé and Oleron, circa 1625). Cardinal Richelieu managed to obtain ships from England and Holland manned by French captains and troops. He placed them under the command of "Montmorency" who drove the rebels from *Rhé* and *Oleron*.

Since no one knew where the tunnel ended, Pepére was certain that he had found the missing end, and swore us all to secrecy. Pepere and I enlarged the opening, made steps out of dirt and stones, and cleared enough rubble to make the tunnel large enough for eight or ten people. By installing posts and support beams we strengthened the existing tunnel. That became our ready made bomb shelter.

A few weeks later the school sent Serge home; the bombing had severely damaged the city of Thouars and all the schools closed. Most of the homes in LaPalice had been flattened, but the quay for the ferry had escaped serious damage. It was still difficult for the boats to cross the short distance since the Germans had laid mines on both sides of the channel.

Each night we celebrated a special ritual. It was quite a production to prepare the house. First I closed the curtains in Mamie's room then brought the blankets. Pepére and Serge hung the blankets over the window and even inside the doorway of the front entrance. Those precautions were more to eliminate sound rather than light. The ownership of working radios was strictly *verbotten* by the German command. Pepére unscrewed the back of the radio. He unwrapped the vacuum tube he had hidden away, and plugged it in. The preparation was finished in time for the nine o'clock opening phrase of Beethoven's Fifth Symphony. The BBC had begun the nightly transmission in French. The broadcast began with "*Les Francais parles aux Francais*!" (The French are speaking to the French!) We sat huddled around the *poste de TSF,* spellbound.

First, there was a message of hope, followed by a positive report on the events of the day. Then came the coded messages, about "green goats" or "Jean's cow needs new clothes". Those words were repeated three times. Undoubtedly important messages for the F.F.I., the French Resistance, but meaningless to us. The broadcast over, Pepére removed the tube, wrapped it cautiously in a linen napkin, and hid it inside a large Chinese vase. We would repeat the process each night.

During the mornings, Pepére went around to the neighbors, telling them of the news we had heard the night before on the illegal TSF. They listened, nodding sagely to his every word, giving him a feeling of great importance.

We had music in the house again. Serge not only played the piano any time during the day that he had the urge, but he also had the gift of bringing the house to life by his story telling. He was a definite relief to me, since I had been living in a dormant house for several months.

Serge and I went to the beach from time to time. Pepére's cousin, Tante Jane had a beach house where we changed into our bathing suits. Serge swam as much as he could in a short time. I had not yet learned, so I sat on the beach and made sand and rock castles. The beach had almost no sand, unless the tide was very low. The rest of the time the entire beach was covered with gray, flat pebbles. They were great for skipping across the water; my record was six skips. Serge could do at least ten.

One of the days at the beach Serge tried to see how long he could stay under water. I counted to well over one hundred. He had become so sure of his ability, that he put me on his back and swam way out over my head. A wave knocked me off his back. He dove time and again but couldn't find me. Fortunately, there were a few adults who saw what happened and they were able to help him fish me out.

I had heard that your life flashed before you. All I had was panic at first, then a warm feeling of comfort. Then again the feeling of panic as I started breathing. I didn't know that I would have that same experience again seven years later.

The beach at the base of the sea wall, was covered with great rolls of barbed wire, topped with a thin layer of kelp. The Germans, placed them there as part of the defenses against an amphibious invasion. The game was to climb up the steep slippery wall. I tried, slid back and fell into the rolls of barbed wire. I still have some scars.

Food was scarce, even on the island, which was a farming and fishing community. The Germans confiscated almost all of the vegetables to send to the front. Serge found bees wax candles that Maman had hidden for emergencies. He took a bite out of one, and then handed it to me to try. Though I was reluctant at first, I was hungry enough to try anything. I bit into it, the texture was not too appealing, but it had a sweet flavor that turned out to be quite a delicacy.

Serge and I foraged for food. We went to the beach to harvest shrimp with wooden framed push nets. We seldom brought in more than ten or twelve at the time. Several drags later we had enough for a meal for the four of us. It was really too bad that the shrimp were only close to the beach for a short season.

Pepére had shown us how to dig for "razor" clams. They were about four inches long and looked like a knife handle. We went to another beach at low tide, each with a basket, and a small can of coarse salt. You looked for two holes in the sand; then placed a grain of salt over each of the holes. Soon the clam squirted water. Carefully you reached down into the sand with thumb and index finger on either side of the clam, and then steadily you pulled it out of its hole.

During one of our shrimping expeditions, Serge stepped on a sea urchin, puncturing his heel. A few days later, his foot had swollen to almost twice-normal size, and he was in tremendous pain. Maman took him to the new nurse in town. She said that he needed a doctor. The old doctor had died and a new one had come to St. Martin.

They rode their bicycles and went to see him at the clinic. He was the first Indo-Chinese doctor on the island. His presence created much controversy and caused a lot of conversation. France was still occupying Indo-China where my godfather Lucien was stationed. There was a serious division of the population. The older people felt that the Germans had brought him to the island to inflict harm on the population. Then the other group believed that he was a doctor who had studied in France, and would honor his oath to administer proper care to the sick, regardless of his heritage.

The Doctor made the decision to keep Serge and to operate the next day. He lanced the abscess on the twenty-ninth of April 1943. The infection was very severe, so the doctor decided to keep him a few days. Pepére borrowed a small donkey powered cart from a neighbor so that we could all pass New Years day at the hospital. The day before Serge was to be released I had gone back to the hospital with Maman. The doctor saw me, said that I looked unhealthy and sounded really bad, so he thought that he should examine me.

Serge left the clinic and I moved into his bed to have my tonsils removed. I was not comfortable with having surgery; in fact I was downright scared. So rather than being placed on the table, the pretty blond nurse held me on her lap for them to administer the chloroform and ether mixture.

The next day Doctor Metzger walked into the ward and stopped at my bed. He had seen my name in the hospital records and remembered me from earlier in the year. He was very kind and told me to have my mother let him know when I was to be released; he would send his car to take me back to La Flotte since the weather was really bad.

I told Maman about my visitor. She decided against accepting the offer; so upon my release we waited an extra day at a cousin's house, then we took the bus.

The town crier would generally come once a week. My grandparents' house was on a corner where he stopped, beat a tattoo on his drum to get the attention of anyone in hearing, then go through his list of announcements. This day was another "stay off the streets" type of warning for the following day. Trucks loaded with soldiers were heading for Sablanceaux early in the morning. There was more activity than we had seen in some time. The Germans were leaving our part of the island.

Dr. Metzger's staff car squealed to a stop at the front door. He knocked loudly. Pepére opened the door to see the usually immaculately groomed doctor, unshaven. The engine was running and his door stayed open, the driver didn't even get out of the car as he usually did. The doctor had taken the time to say goodbye. He and the rest of the island garrison were being transferred to the "front". Even though he got mad at me, I would miss him. We heard much later that he had been captured and taken to England.

We had become accustomed to the soldiers in town. Though they were the enemy, they were a pretty good sort. They didn't stand for interference from the local population, but they seemed to be pretty fair. They were the older more experienced soldiers, and they did not necessarily embrace the Nazi party line. They were eager to talk about their families and show photographs. They were quick to say that they hoped for a rapid end to the war, so they could go home to their families.

A small group stayed behind, until the new detachment arrived. It was like night and day. Some of the officers remained to be in charge of the replacements. The new soldiers were much younger, some in their teens. They never smiled, and they were pretty pushy.

The bombing became more frequent and much more intense. The town crier came again with the word that any Frenchman aiding a downed allied pilot would be shot. That really didn't deter anyone. The rule had been in effect for months, without being followed. Many farmers and fishermen were heroes who rescued and hid our friends. Though they never received much credit, if any, they did have the knowledge and satisfaction that they had been a part of the liberation.

The town crier came around again. This time it was to give the word that the Allies were going to bomb the island. All residents would have to leave. Most of the bombing before had been across our channel on the mainland. The choice now, was to send children and seniors to stay with friends on the mainland or to be sent to camp-like colonies.

It was extremely difficult to find a place to stay among friends. Most were in worse shape than we were. All the food went to the Germans except for the part people hid under threat of being shot. Now the rule was by fear; the words of the times were "do it or be shot."

Pepére had lived on *Ile de Ré* almost all of his life. His home had been his father's. He said he wasn't going anywhere! If he was going to die it was better to die in his home with his wife, than in an unfamiliar place with strangers. So he told my mother to take us and leave.

The priest in La Flotte had been working on finding a place for me to hide since I arrived on the island. Normally it didn't take too long to find a farm family willing to care for a city child. My case was different; it was not simply to give me a home and feed me, it was also to hide me from the Gestapo. They didn't want to expose their families to possible arrest, or worse. Finally *Monsieur le Curé* and the group from Paris, working together through another priest, found a family in the village of Siecq who would take me in for as long as needed. Siecq was in the department of Charente approximately half way between St. Jean D'Angely and Angoulême.

We had to leave immediately. Maman didn't want to leave Pepére and Mamie alone on the island so she devised a method for Serge to stay with them until she returned from taking me to Siecq.

A farmer was to employ him as an "essential" hand to help with his crops. The Germans needed the crops so he was allowed to stay.

I had a bout with jaundice that kept me from going with the rest of the village children. Ten days or so later we said a tearful farewell; each of us certain that we would never see the other again. Maman and I took the ferry to La Palice, and walked to La Rochelle. We stayed in the beautiful rail station waiting for a train to Angoulême. Railroad tracks had been bombed the day before so all trains in that area were canceled. Maman had friends there so we spent the night in La Rochelle with them.

The next morning we walked back to the station and again heard that trains were not running. There was a lot of German troop movement. Maman's German was very fluent. In passing a truck she overheard that they were going to St. Jean D'Angely. That was in the direction we wanted to go. Very casually, in German she asked for a ride for both of us. Surprisingly they agreed. We climbed in the back of the truck and huddled against the chill. Two of the soldiers unrolled their blankets and covered us. I slept most of the way, still weak from the jaundice.

I remember going to the hotel in St. Jean D'Angely when we arrived, planning to spend the night, and to set out the next day. First we would try to catch a train, but I had no doubt that we would arrive, even if we had to walk.

We were checking in when a lady came in asking the owner for us. Maman introduced herself and asked why she wanted us. She had received a letter from her mother on *Ile de Ré* telling her that we would be passing through St. Jean D'Angely, and to try to make us comfortable. We went without hesitation and were treated to a good farm meal. The fare was the first chicken we had seen in months, served with bread and homemade jam. All I could eat though, was the bread and jam. It's amazing how much the stomach can shrink while suffering from malnutrition.

We visited, and gave her news of the people on *Ile de Ré*. The next day was to be long. Not knowing what to expect we went to bed and really slept. I was awakened by the wail of the air raid sirens. Almost immediately bombs dropped all around us shaking the house. Dust from the ceiling fell in my face, and I pulled the feather comforter over my head to shut out the noise and to gain a little safety. Next, we heard the rhythmic klaxon of the fire trucks. We almost never heard one without the other. We were so accustomed to those sounds, and I was so tired that I went back to sleep anyway.

Breakfast consisted of a large bowl of warm milk and bread. We expressed our appreciation and said our good-byes. We then walked to the railroad station to see if the trains were running to *Angouleme*. We had to pass in front of the hotel where we would have stayed. Only a heap of rubble remained. Plumes of smoke were still dancing in front of the firemen's hoses. We had been saved again. Why?

Undoubtedly, there had been a number of people like us in the hotel who were not so fortunate. We stopped, and said a small prayer of thanks for ourselves and for the souls of the hotel guests. Maman's hands began to tremble; the strain of running seemed to be taking its toll. The train was operating that day and we boarded. It took a few hours to clear the tracks from the air raid, but we were under way. Two hours later we reached our destination... the village named Siecq.

Journey Three

Ile de Ré to Siecq

Chapter Seven

Siecq was a typical small farming village located in the Cognac country. It was very neat and clean, as long as it did not rain. We had very little trouble finding the house of Monsieur and Madame Paul Mechain. The people we asked for directions were anxious to point out their large house, almost as if their knowing the location made them friends of important people.

We pulled the bell wire announcing our arrival. The garden gate was through a stone wall, separating their courtyard and the street. An elderly lady opened the gate; she was expecting us. She put her arms around me crying "here is Guy, here is Guy". She led us to the kitchen where she was preparing a pot roast with carrots and potatoes. You can't imagine our excitement. This was the first time we had seen beef in months.

Madame Mechain apologized for Monsieur Mechain who was in the fields, and would return later. Mademoiselle Anne Marie, their middle aged daughter was at church where she usually spent a good portion of each day.

Madame Mechain showed us upstairs where we were to sleep. The house was a typical one hundred and fifty-year-old stone farmhouse with a slate roof, furnished in the usual country style. We were assigned to a large bedroom decorated with velvet drapes and gold embroidered silk wall hangings. Now that was not typical. The formal parts of the home were decorated with artifacts that their son Jean had brought or sent, from all over the world.

That evening, after going upstairs, I visualized Jean in several fascinating roles. He was an officer in the Foreign Legion like my Godfather Lucien. Another, that he was the owner of a famous circus that toured the world. He would come back to visit soon and I would go with him as an apprentice animal trainer. Later, to my dismay, I found out that Jean was "only" a ship's Captain, in the Merchant Marine. It seemed strange that he was seldom mentioned and that I never saw him.

The first night was so peaceful. Sounds of the war were left behind us. The next morning, all reminders of the war seemed gone. We had all the milk and bread we wanted for breakfast.

Maman and I set out to find the school, overlooking the town square close to the bakery. We introduced ourselves to the director and his wife, both were teachers. I was assigned a seat at one of the two tables in a class of fourteen. The introductions were very superficial, something like "Class this is Guy". Later, I found out that there were two other children from *Ile de Ré*, but they were not there for the same reason. Their parents had found families on their own who, for a monthly fee would board them. This would insure their safety and their well being as well as appeasing their hunger.

There were only a few weeks of school left before vacation. I had missed a lot due to my illness, but I was enrolled anyway, to become familiar with the school and the teachers. They would work with me to catch up with my class, by giving Mademoiselle Mechain enough lessons for me to last throughout the summer.

Maman only stayed a few days since she was going back to the island to be with Serge and my grandparents. I was determined to be strong and not cry during our good-byes. I remembered that Dr. Eva had said that all this would help make me strong. Anyway, I was seven years old now.

The day after Maman left, Mademoiselle Marie called me into the living room. I was a bit apprehensive. Looking around the room I saw a menagerie of stuffed birds and animals. A large elephant tusk leaned in a corner. She pointed to a stool made from a stuffed elephant's foot for me to sit on.

Mademoiselle Mechain was not unkind but she was very stern. I was never to go to this room or the bedroom where Maman and I had slept, unless she was with me. I would now sleep in her room on a small cot placed against the wall. I would go to mass with her every morning, and vespers twice a week. On Sunday I would go to six o'clock and eleven o'clock mass. Then there was catechism, I think it was on Thursday, the day we had no school.

I was sure to get enough prayers credited to me, and that my place in heaven was secure, no matter how long I lived. She said that I was to call her Amie (as in friend) and not Mademoiselle. I would be assigned certain duties in a few days.

We spent the rest of the day visiting the grounds, the stables, the winery, and the distillery where the Cognac was made and finally another house they owned a block away, directly in front of the post office. This day had been very tiring, whether physical or mental I don't know, but I slept in my new bed "like an angel" Amie had told her mother at breakfast, after Mass.

There was no school the next day, so Monsieur Mechain took me with him to visit his farms where other families lived and cared for his fields and vineyards. We rode in a large *charrette* pulled by a great white horse named “Papillon”. I thought it was a funny name for him, he was far from being a butterfly.

Mr. Mechain was not very talkative and neither was I. There were questions I wanted to ask but I didn’t dare disturb him. The rest of that year I spent mostly with Amie and at school.

My assigned chores were to feed the rabbits, chickens, ducks and the geese; gather the eggs and keep the graveled courtyard clean. The rabbits were fun and I didn’t mind the chickens. Amie warned me about one big gander, the lord of the geese. She told me that he would flap his wings, attacking me, trying to get all the corn. He was almost as tall as me with his neck stretched out. At first I would try to meet him head on but he managed to chase me around until I slipped then fell in a barnyard full of goose droppings. Now there’s an experience! I went back to the house looking a bit worse for wear. I walked in just in time for everyone to laugh at me. I thought to myself, “goose, this is the last time that you make me look foolish!” The next day I picked up a stick and beat the tin pan like a drum while I started chasing him, I emptied the corn in the old dishpan and went on my way, very pleased with myself.

That experience taught me that if you work up enough courage to knock on the fire breathing dragon’s door, you will probably find out, that he isn’t as fearsome as the fire and smoke would lead you to believe. That lesson has stood me in good stead throughout my life. It’s amazing what you can credit to goose droppings.

A small stream flowed through the field just outside the garden where the fowl ran free. One day I ran back to the house telling Amie that a hen was drowning. It was the mother of a brood of ducks. The female duck had died, so they placed the duck eggs under a setting hen to hatch. The ducklings went swimming and mama hen tried to follow. Amie arrived just in time to pull her out. Later mama hen did drown when no one was around to save her.

Serge came to visit during school vacation, while Maman was in Paris working. I showed him around town. In the square in front of the church the old men played "boule" a French version of "Boccie Ball". I took him out to one of the fields where I had found an abandoned pigeon coop. It was big enough for us to use as a fort. We spent quite a few hours there jousting at windmills and planning the overthrow of the German army.

Even though Serge was there, I still had to go to church every day. At first Serge went too. He had been an altar boy so he could serve mass with me. One Sunday he was playing the organ before mass and *Monsieur le Curé* asked him to play during mass. He played much better than Amie. After that he no longer had to go to church every day, just one mass on Sunday. Amie, somewhat hurt that she had been partially replaced, still played at the other masses. She appeared a little cooler toward Serge after that.

One of the boys that I had met at school worked on his family's farm. They were bringing water in a horse drawn tank wagon, to irrigate the field when he fell off the wagon. One of the large wooden wheels of the heavy wagon ran over him, killing him. The village came to a halt. It was bad enough when an old member of the community died, but he was so young. The shops were drapped in black. I was the altar boy at the funeral, since in the short time I had been there the priest found out I was the only one who didn't cry at funerals. Before he disappeared, my father taught me that crying was not only a visible display of emotion, but also a sign of weakness. Therefore it should not be a part of a man's life. So I worked very hard at not crying. If a tear did flow I was upset at myself for days.

Vacation over, Serge went back to school in Thouars, this time without any undue events, not even a train bombing.

School started for us again. I developed a friendship with two different boys. One was the son of the postmistress, his name was Jacques also, like my friend in Paris; the other was the son of the blacksmith, Philippe.

One afternoon after school Jacques and I walked down the street adjacent to the post office. That street dwindled into a country lane, which eventually ended in a field a few hundred meters away. Not far from the tree line, was a strange wagon. It looked like a red box with yellow wheels and black automobile tires; windows and a smokestack. It reminded me of the pictures I had seen of horse drawn gypsy wagons. We thought it looked abandoned so we went closer. We were almost up to it when a man opened the door and smiled at us. He came out and sat on the steps and spoke to us with a strange accent.

He asked who we were, and what we were doing? What we did after school and who our friends were. He became excited when he heard that Jacques was the son of the postmistress. He split a pomegranate in two and gave us each half. Neither of us had ever seen one before and didn't know exactly what to do with it. He showed us, then asked us to come back the next day.

We went back to the post office and told his mother all about our new friend. She warned us about strangers, stressing that she didn't want us to go back. The next day we obeyed her grudgingly and discussed our position. Since we had told him that we would return, we should. Then again we had to obey our parents. We rationalized that since Jacques' mother was not my mother it would be all right if I went. Jacques on the other hand insisted that I could not go alone, it wasn't prudent. He went along to insure that I was safe.

I felt that he was simply as curious as I was; so we made up our minds to go back the next day. We would face the consequences later. I felt that I just had to go, my father had taught me to honor my commitments. His lessons weren't always spelled out in simple words, sometimes they were illustrated by Aesop's fables, other times by posing hypothetical problems for me to solve. In any case I usually arrived at the necessary conclusions.

Our new friend was a little bit curt when he greeted us. He expected us the day before and didn't hesitate to let us know he was disappointed. We explained our predicament, and then he said that he understood, but still he had worried about us. He said that to make up for disappointing him we should deliver a folded piece of paper to Jacques' mother. He cautioned us not to read it. Our feelings were hurt; we certainly would have helped him without being made to feel guilty.

Our nameless friend stayed in the house on wheels at least two months. Once a week on different days Jacques' mother would give us letters to take to the "gypsy". They were never in an envelope, just folded small. We were never invited in, but we heard noises coming from inside.

The empty house that Monsieur Mechain owned across the street from the post office had been taken over by the Germans to use as the local *Kommandanture*; their headquarters in Siecq. A guard was stationed in front at all times. His wooden hut was positioned on the main street, but also in a way that he could see down the street where we ran to see our friend. I'm sure that the guards became accustomed to seeing us run, and probably didn't think much of it.

Jacques lived with his mother in the back of the post office. He and I would wander around in the fields, doing important things that boys have been doing for centuries, throwing rocks at birds, trying to catch fish with our bare hands, and more important, making slingshots.

Though Jacques and I shared a close friendship, I would occasionally go to the blacksmith shop on the other side of the village to play with Philippe. His father had seen the sling shot I made with Jacques and laughed at it. The fork was crooked and bent back. He said I would never hit a bird with that. One day when we arrived after school he gave me a new one that he had made. It was really a beauty. It was made of heavy wire with strips from an old inner tube. He had also made triangular pieces of flat iron to use as projectiles instead of rocks. I could hit almost everything I wanted with that one. Of course, Philippe had one just like it.

Late one afternoon we returned from a bird hunt when from behind the large blackberry thicket in front of the blacksmith shop we saw a German officer astride his horse. He was making arrangements to have the horse shod. His tone sounded so harsh as he spoke to Philippe's father. We didn't like it. We stayed hidden behind the thicket got our slingshots ready and shot the horse in the flank and in the rump. The horse reared almost throwing the German, he managed to get his horse under control and we shot him again. This time the horse ran. I don't know how long it took him to get the horse stopped, since we ran in the other direction as fast as we could, while trying to stay hidden. I don't believe that the German saw us, if he did he decided not to do anything about it.

The *vendange*, (harvesting of the grapes) took over the daily life for a few short weeks. Everyone who could pick grapes went to the vineyards, including me. I would pick for awhile; fill my basket then go empty it in the barrels on the four wheeled wagon. That wagon was really a sight. A few months before the Germans had come through rounding up all but one horse per farm. So Monsieur Mechain had Papillon teamed with an ox to pull the heavy wagon. They had learned to pull together pretty well, except when the ox decided to go in a different direction from the horse. Papillon would then try to kick his partner. When I became tired, I was assigned the task of staying on the wagon to pick up the grapes that fell on the wagon floor, and on the ground, during the dumping of baskets.

The barrels full, we drove the wagon to the winery. There, two men dumped the grapes into the large hand operated press. When the press was full thick planks were placed on top of the grapes. A ratcheted fitting that accommodated a long iron handle was matched with a vertical worm gear. At first one man would walk around the threaded center connection. As the grapes compressed the juice flowed into a cement pit. Later the juice was pumped into huge wooden vats with open tops.

The grape harvest finished one of the most unpleasant tasks was to skim the foam from the top of the vats. Monsieur Mechain hired a tall, cadaverous man to take care of the eight huge vats. As the fermentation process progressed, he would start in the morning and skim all the vats; and in the evening he would do it again. One vat was much larger than the others; he had to skim standing on a plank that went across the vat. One morning he didn't show up for the breakfast Madame Mechain had prepared. Lunch came, he wasn't there either. Monsieur Mechain went to look for him but couldn't find him. The next morning he still had not returned.

Somebody had to skim the vats and Monsieur Mechain was too old. He found someone else to do it. The story told to us was that the hand had left to rejoin his family in another village. But a few weeks later the rumor circulating was, that while the new skimmer was doing his job, he plunged his dipper deep in the biggest vat and found the body. Apparently the regular skimmer had either slipped or had been overcome by fumes and fallen in the vat. The funeral was held in another village, and the police was not even involved. No one from the farm went to a funeral.

Monsieur Mechain and his brother-in-law had a heated discussion in the kitchen that went on into the night; encouraged by the consumption of several bottles of *gros rouge*. I was in our room upstairs in the other side of the house and could not hear the topic of conversation, only the occasional raised voice. Later I did find out, that wine from that vat was to be placed in marked kegs. When bottled it was to be sold only to the Germans.

Chapter Eight

The underground activity grew in the area. The FFI (*Force Francaise Interieur*) did a lot to confuse and irritate the Germans who seemed to be losing some of their control. Posters with the ever-present German eagle and swastika were placed all over town. They started with "*Achtung*!" in large type; the message in the body commanded citizens who owned guns to turn them in at city hall and it finished with the usual closing of "*Heil Hitler*!"

A farm community like Siecq had its share of hunters who scorned the words on the posters. Give up their guns? Never! The success of the drive was dismal. French law required all guns to be registered at city hall, so it was a simple matter for the German soldiers to go to each house on the registration list and demand the surrender of the weapons. A few people had the audacity to deny having them. Supposedly they had been sold, lost in the fields, or given to an out of town relative. Any excuse was used. The German Commandant, infuriated by the lack of cooperation, had a number of men on the list arrested and taken to the town jail. Later we heard that some had been shot. We also heard that in other villages recalcitrant gun owners weren't taken to prison at all but were marched directly to the Town Square, placed against the wall and immediately shot by a firing squad. Monsieur Mechain turned over his beautiful German "drilling" but kept the unregistered .22 rifle his son had brought from an early voyage.

The next edict was to turn all horses in to the *Kommandantur* in Angoulême. Monsieur Mechain tried in vain to keep his "Papillon". He took a few bottles of Cognac to the Commandant in Siecq; even that didn't work. He and I hitched Papillon to an old leather topped carriage while Madame Mechain prepared a lunch for our trip. The ride would last almost eight hours, although it was only around forty kilometers.

We were not the only ones taking horses to Angoulême. Instead of herding the horses together and letting a few people take them all, each owner had to declare and cede his property in person. Once on the road we fell in place joining a rag-tag assortment of horse drawn carts. The convoy stopped by the side of the road just before arriving in the town of Rouillac. We brought out our napkin-wrapped, lunches and the essential bottle of red wine. Pleasantries were exchanged between travelers during the meal, and then the tenor of the discussions went quickly from dissatisfaction of the government to anger at the Germans. All the possessions they or their parents had worked for, were slowly being confiscated by the invaders. It seemed that they all felt something should be done, but no one knew what or how.

I looked around at the lunch group, realizing we were all men or boys. Though we were on the main road from La Rochelle to Angoulême, there was little traffic that day. We were preparing to get under way when the red Gypsy wagon from our field pulled along side the group. My friend had been coming from the direction we were going. He was not alone, a very dark complexioned woman wearing a babushka sat next to him. My friend didn't see me. He asked why the group was there and where we were going. One of the men assumed the role of spokesman and told him of our predicament. With his accent the Gypsy spoke passionately about "*les boches*", his listeners all nodded sagely in agreement. The gypsy spotted me, raised his hand and started to speak, then changed his mind and waved goodbye to all.

The group spokesman whom I didn't know came over to our carriage. He was a big man with a cigarette-burned, red mustache and muddy knee-high black boots, the perfect illustration of a storybook "ogre". He glanced at Monsieur Mechain then focused on me. "So you're the one!" he said. I was apprehensive and had no idea why he said that. I looked at him, then at Monsieur Mechain, shaking my head in confusion. The "ogre" told Monsieur Mechain, pointing a pudgy finger at me, "He's the one taking the messages to the gypsy for the underground". Monsieur Mechain looked down at me, asking if this was true. I told him yes but I was not alone. Jacques' mother had told us not to say anything to anyone about what we did, so how did he know?

Evidently the "ogre" had seen the beginning of the Gypsy's gesture and then had assumed a lot. He turned around to the group and said with pride "this is the little one who has been taking messages to the F.F.I. At least he is doing something!" They didn't say anything as almost in unison they looked down at their shoes. They raised their hands as in a wave more than in a salute, but they waited for us to take our place. This time we were the second carriage of the convoy behind the "ogre".

During the few months I had lived with the Mechain family I had only seen Monsieur angry once. His ox, the harness partner of Papillon, stepped on his foot and broke it. I had now seen him angry again. Monsieur Mechain waited until we were underway before he started.

"We are hiding you from the Germans and you are to keep out of sight. So what do you do? You take messages to the underground! Do you realize you could be shot? I could lose my farm, in fact I could be shot!" The tirade went on for some time. That was my first real "chewing out". I knew that Monsieur Mechain was right, but I was crushed. I bit the inside of my lip to keep from crying. I was proud of that, even though I had to swallow the blood in my mouth.

We arrived in Angoulême late in the afternoon and couldn't turn Papillon over to the Germans until the next day. Monsieur Mechain drove us to his cousin's house for the night. After a good meal, Monsieur Mechain went to the stable and spent most of the evening currying and brushing the big white horse. We didn't know if he was to be a workhorse or if he would be turned into horse sausage. We both hoped against hope but had very little faith. He was a handsome workhorse but just wouldn't look right with a saddle. He had been such an important part of the farm and had an excellent temperament.

I went to bed and for the first time in several months I was awakened by the high pitched wail of the now unfamiliar air raid sirens. Almost immediately bombs exploded too close for comfort. There was a large detachment of German soldiers in Angoulême, so this may have been an intentional target. The sirens stopped as soon as the drone of bomber engines faded from earshot; but the night was just beginning. Within minutes smaller explosions resounded in the streets. The FFI had taken advantage of the bombing to detonate small bombs or grenades. Running hobnailed boots sounded on the cobbled street followed by the terrifying sound of rifle buts slamming on doors just a few houses away.

Monsieur Mechain came into my dark room, scooped me from my bed and almost ran down the stairs, stumbling on the next to last step. He caught himself to keep from falling but dropped me in the process. By then I was wide-awake. He pulled my hand, jerking me down the sloping cellar. His cousin had preceded us with a lantern; still it was a dark, dank, kind of a root cellar. Several potato sacks were stacked two across alternately in one corner. A mound of loose potatoes was piled adjacent to the sacks for daily use, lime sprinkled on top to preserve them. In another corner beets and rutabagas were piled together.

Monsieur Mechain opened an empty burlap sack and helped me climb in. He pushed me down and then pulled the sides up over my head and tied it closed like the others. He pulled one sack toward him and laid me down on top of the pile against the wall. He told me to lie there, stay quiet and not to move until he came in the room to say that it was over. The door to the cellar closed, leaving me in complete darkness.

I lay there as if in a cocoon for what seemed like hours. It wasn't long before I started hearing small noises that I could not readily identify, some kind of rustling. I heard gnawing from the direction of the sugar beets. Soon I felt something running across my sack, over my shoulders. Sharp claws penetrated the weave of the sack scratching my cheek. That's when I realized that I was sharing my hiding place with rats.

I had never really been afraid of animals, not even mice, but I had never had a first-hand experience with rats. I told myself that I was inside a sack and they could not bite me. But it was really difficult to lie there without moving, particularly since I was in the dark cellar alone. I tried dozing in my cramped position, but the earthen smell of the vegetables punctuated by the odor of an occasional rotting potato was nauseating and burning my eyes. I roused fully, really uncomfortable lying on my lumpy bed.

I heard voices and through the weave of my sack I saw the glow of a lantern. I heard Monsieur Mechain in halting German telling someone that this was only the vegetable cellar. I heard the clank of gas mask container hitting something metallic, then a sort of a grunt. The bag in front of me was pushed into me moving me back against the wall. As quickly as they had arrived, the footsteps retreated back up the stairs.

Within minutes Monsieur Mechain came back down and pulled the sack down around me allowing me to step out of it. He put his arms around me and held me for a few seconds. That surprised me. That was the only time that he had ever shown any kind of affection. Of course it might have been sheer relief. It wasn't until later on the way home that he told me the German soldier had stuck his bayonet in several sacks, including the one in front of me. We went back upstairs; within minutes I was back asleep.

The next morning Monsieur Mechain and I went to the stable where he left the carriage while he led "Papillon" out of the gate. I could see the tears in his eyes. Brusquely he told me to go back in the house and stay with the relatives until he returned. He didn't want to take a chance with me at the Germans' compound.

He came back to the house around noon but didn't eat. Silently, we walked to the train station and arrived in time for the train to Siecq.

The next day I rushed to find Jacques to tell him that I had seen the Gypsy wagon. I found him in the back of the post office, his mother preparing another letter. Excitedly he told me that the Gypsy was back at the same instant that I was telling him of my adventure.

The letter ready, Jacques' mother told us to go, "Hurry and come right back". We ran out of the side door as usual. The sentry at the gate of the Mechain house saw us and told us to "halt" we thought he was only joking with us so we kept on running. Almost immediately as we rounded a curve in the street, a rifle shot rang out and a bullet hit the wall above our heads, sending a shower of rock fragments all over me. We looked back but he was still by his guard post so we kept going.

We arrived in the clearing where the wagon had been but saw nothing. We looked around the same vicinity and eventually found his wagon parked in the woods by a small stream. His donkeys were tied to a tree with a long rope instead of roaming in the fields.

He welcomed us and talked about his trip. He had been outside of Limoge for a few weeks, but he had been sent back to Siecq. The lady I had seen with him on the road came out of the house wagon. She looked different this time; the babushka was gone then I realized her face was not dark at all. She had long black hair that went straight down to the middle of her back. She offered us a glass of white wine that had not yet fermented.

The gypsy went back in the wagon and came out with a small flat package. He called me closer and lifted the back of my school smock and tied the package around my waist in the small of my back. He rubbed the top of my head like a puppy, then placed a hand behind each of us and gave us a push. "Go back to the post office and deliver this right away."

A few days later we went back with a letter. The wagon was there but the donkeys were gone. We knocked on the door; there was no answer. We knocked harder and this time the blows opened the unlatched door. The place was a mess. The bedclothes were on the floor and drawers had been pulled out from a built in chest and dumped on the bed. The glass chimney from the oil lamp lay broken in pieces on the floor by an inverted basket. We knew that something really bad must have happened. The dried food on the plates made us think that no one had been there in a few days so we hurried back to the post office, a long way around.

That afternoon I told Monsieur Mechain that we had gone back to see the Gypsy, that his house was still there but we had been unable to find him. Monsieur Mechain exploded. He called me "some kind of idiot". He thought I had understood when we spoke the last time that I was not to go back. He calmed himself a little and told me that he had heard the Germans had taken the Gypsy and a woman prisoner only three days before. He seemed to withdraw in thought, then exclaimed, "The time has arrived, come with me"!

I followed Monsieur Mechain to the wash shed that was attached to the side of main house. A large stone sink was next to a cement trough, in line with a cement cistern built high enough to supply gravity fed running water to the rest of the house.

The well had been dug over a century ago and was beautifully lined with stones and mortar. It still had the cross frame with the large cast iron pulley used to bring up buckets of water. The hand pump mounted on the outside of the well topped a lead pipe going down inside the wall past the water level. A wooden platform almost the diameter of the well had been built of heavy planks. A bridle fashioned from three ropes and attached to a chain allowed the platform to be raised and lowered. The ladies of the family for the last two generations had used it to keep butter, milk, cheese and eggs cool in the summer.

Monsieur Mechain cranked the platform up almost to the top and locked the handle in place with a rope loop. He removed the perishables, then told me to climb onto the platform. Apprehension swept over me. I knew that I was to be punished by being sent down the well on the platform. How long I would stay I didn't know. I knew that I had disobeyed him, but what I had done I felt it was my duty to do. I had done it for *La Belle France*. I was sorry to have disobeyed Monsieur Mechain, but I rationalized that he had not made it clear; anyway I probably would do the same thing again. This punishment seemed a bit extreme but Monsieur Mechain was not the kind of man that you challenged. I kept quiet and climbed onto the platform.

The platform tilted a little making me grab for the rope as he began lowering me. He said in a surprisingly kind voice "Look all around you. When you see a small cave in the wall tell me". As he lowered me, I could feel the drop in temperature and the increase in humidity. The stonework was really fine, hardly what you would expect to find in a well. The flat stones were almost identical in size. It had taken a true artisan to do this.

The light was diminishing and the staleness of the air was almost nauseating. He lowered the platform further until I saw a small grotto in the wall. I was probably five or six meters down and the light was really bad. I called out to Monsieur Mechain, but he didn't seem to hear me and kept lowering. I almost screamed at him to stop. "I see something". That time he heard me.

He called down to me to climb into the grotto. The platform tilted a little more with my shifting weight, I held on to the rope bridle for dear life, but I managed to do it. It was large enough for me to sit on my heels with my head bowed, and deep enough for the width of my shoulders but hardly more. I doubted that an adult could have hidden there. There certainly was no place to sit upright unless I dangled my legs down the well, and I was too scared to do that. The water was still a good way down. Monsieur

Mechain called down for me to get back on the platform so he could lift me back out.

I was really confused. If that had been my punishment, it really had not been that bad. As before, I was accustomed to small places and that had not bothered me. Just my ego was bruised. I was up and out in less than a minute. He sat me down on the edge of the well and then recounted the story of the cave. Years before, when his grandfather owned the house and he was approximately my age, a small part of the well had crumbled. Rather than replacing new dirt to make the wall flush a mason had descended on a platform; reshaped the hole and lined the grotto with stone. That platform gave his father the idea for the cooler.

He went on to tell me that if the Gestapo came looking for me, he would quickly lower me down the well for me to get into the cave. Then they would raise the platform and replace the perishables. I was to stay there until he called down to me that all was clear for me to return. He cautioned me that I would have to stay back as far as possible and make myself small. The Germans always looked down wells and usually dropped stones to hear the water splash making sure that a false floor had not been constructed deep in the well. The French have used wells as hiding places for centuries. After this explanation, he cautioned me and made me promise that I would never reveal this hiding place.

That night I lay in bed wondering how many children my age had to go through as many precautions simply to stay alive and free. I wondered again why all these people were kind enough and concerned enough to see that I stayed safe.

The next morning I ran to the post office to tell Jacques what I had heard about the Gypsy. His mother had told him the same thing earlier. We talked about it at length, wondering who he really was and who the lady was. It dawned on us that the day the German shot over our heads, someone must have followed us, then returned and captured him. We felt terrible. We had not wanted that to happen. We never saw him nor heard about him again.

For a long time, I had nightmares about being there when they were captured. I once dreamt that I had been arrested and sent to the camp where my father was being detained. I saw him briefly, hunched over, shuffling endlessly around the perimeter of the men's compound. I started to call out "Papa", but before the word was out of my mouth, a woman knocked me to the ground telling me to keep quiet. Calling out was forbidden under penalty of death.

A barbed wire fence separated the men from the women and children. The two groups walked along the perimeters of their respective compounds in opposite direction; converging at the fence in the hope that one could recognize a friend or loved one. Occasionally one could see hands desperately reaching for each other across the wire barrier. The pain from cuts and scratches were ignored for an instant of touch. Amie would wake me and take me on her bed with her and cover me; but she never allowed me to sleep in her bed as Doctor Eva had.

Thanks to the sisters in La Flotte school went well for me. I already knew my multiplication tables. The rest of the children in my class were just learning them. A pretty girl with big eyes and long dark ringlets was having a terrible time learning hers. I can truly say that I was smitten. Therése was my first love. I offered to help her in her studies.

Her parents had a large farm on the opposite side of town from us. We spent a lot of time smiling at each other in class, and I would look for any excuse to visit her at home. One day, in the garden house where we studied, she tired of multiplication tables rather quickly and asked if I wanted to play doctor. I had never played, but I was willing to learn. That was my first detailed study in female anatomy.

I came home after our game and found many unfamiliar people in the house. Amie was crying and I was taken in the front room downstairs to see Madame Mechain. No one had thought to tell me that she had died. I had seen a number of dead people after bombings in Paris, but never anyone that I knew. It was quite a shock. Still she looked only as if she was sleeping peacefully.

I was only in the room a few minutes when a stern lady that I didn't know ushered me out. I went to the garden and sat on a stone bench wondering what the loss of Madame Mechain would mean to the family, and particularly to me. Would I be sent away to another house or even to a colony? I became angry with myself for being concerned about my welfare when I should be wondering if she was really going to heaven. She probably would, I rationalized, since she had been a good lady. The priest had discussed death in catechism. From what he had said though, only the very pure went straight to heaven. So I really did not know her fate. If she had sinned earlier in life, she would probably have to go to Purgatory for a few hundred years.

The more I thought, the more uncomfortable I became. I realized that God must have been angry because Therése and I had played doctor even though I knew it was wrong. I was certain that he punished me by letting Madame Mechain die. Her death had to be my fault. I would have to go to confession Saturday afternoon, but how was I going to tell the priest what Therése and I had done? What would my penance be?

I didn't go to confession on Saturday; I simply couldn't get up the nerve. Sunday morning came and I had to serve mass, so of course I had to go to communion. At the last possible minute I asked the priest to hear my confession. He said that he would do it in the sacristy just before mass. I shook like a leaf in the wind; waiting had been so stupid because I would not even have the benefit of the dark confessional in which to hide my shame. Hesitantly I told the priest of our transgression. He turned his head looking down, trying to keep from smiling as he chastised me soundly, told me to never do that again until I was married. He then sentenced me to one Act of Contrition, two Our Fathers and ten Hail Mary's and then to reflect at length on my actions. That penance has stayed with me all my life.

A few days after the funeral, Amie took over all the duties of the house.

Chapter Nine

Christmas of 1943 was almost upon us. Several of us had to prepare the church for midnight mass. Amie sewed new vestments for the priest. I had to stand on a stool and dust all the Stations of the Cross.

Amie taught me to fatten goose livers to make *pâté de foie gras*. Every day, she boiled corn in an iron cauldron, on an open wood fire. While waiting for the corn to boil, she would ask me about my day; my studies at school and what I did on the way home. Then we talked either about what I learned in catechism, or about ancient buildings and their parts. She was taking correspondence courses on Roman architecture. She had a special interest in columns and gargoyles.

The feeding, really the stuffing, of the geese was accomplished by straddling them while on her knees, then inserting a special funnel down their throats. My job was to pour the warm corn in the funnel and turn the handle of the built in auger, forcing the corn down their throats. She would then take her hand and smooth the corn down the gooses' neck. We did around two dozen geese every day for several weeks.

Late one evening, after finishing my part of the process, I encountered Monsieur Mechain pulling a large glass jar out of a hole in the ground. I saw that it was full of money. He tried to turn around to hide it from me, but it was too late. Since he realized that I had seen him, he told me that whenever the French government issued new currency, he would take a bill of each denomination and place it in his jar. He said that only he, and now I, knew the burial place, and never to tell anyone. I now knew three of his secrets. The jar may still be there.

Amie and I celebrated Christmas Eve by going to Midnight Mass. We bundled up, not so much for the walk to church, as for the duration of the mass. The unheated, stone, country church was packed with parishioners. It was beautifully decorated, there were no flowers but the verdure was placed with care and love. The congregation sang, and the priest gave an emotional sermon, pleading for the war to end. Mass over, the church emptied without the usual socializing, so common to the Sunday Mass.

The brisk walk back home took all of ten minutes. Amie heated milk on the ever burning stove, all the while quizzing me about Christmas hymns. She wanted to know which one I could sing for the eleven o'clock mass in the morning. I had thought that midnight mass was going to be the service for the Holy Day. I was wrong. As a seven year old I was blessed with a better than average soprano voice. We decided that I knew the "Cantique de Noel" best. Therefore I would sing the solo.

The long day and warm milk was a bit much for me. My head touched the pillow and I was asleep.

I awoke while it was still dark. I was completely disoriented. Somehow I had switched ends in my bed and was facing the wrong way. I reversed myself and put my head back on the pillow, then my eyes popped open. My mind started wandering, covering a multitude of topics. There was no Christmas tree to look forward to. The last one I had seen was in Paris two years before. We had been invited to the home of the girl who lived in the big house, behind the iron fence, on Rue de la Tourelle. It had been a big beautiful tree, with small, lighted candles at the end of each branch. It must have been a tremendous fire hazard.

That Christmas, *Père Noël* brought me my electric train. The one I could play with, only if my father was there with me. I really missed playing with that train but above that, I really missed my father. I knew my mother had told me once that he might return after the war, then later she had said that he might never return. Regardless of what she had said, I wanted him there, then, to be part of our Christmas.

I had never sung a solo before, and we had not practiced. Amie probably thought that since I sang loudly with others it should be simple. It was not! My mouth dried out and my voice cracked. Thankfully, the priest began to sing along with me. I was so ashamed! I had let Amie down. On the walk home she said that maybe I would do better next Christmas.

The other two children from school had gone back to *Ile de Ré* to spend Christmas with their families. I had been told that they were not in Siecq for the same reason as I, so it was all right for them to return. The Gestapo had no interest in them. They were free to travel without danger of being arrested and deported.

Amie and her father were very good to me. I had friends but they would be with their families. We ate a simple meal, then talked about Madame Mechain and how much she was missed.

The next few months were uneventful. School went on. I had to go to the shoemaker. I had worn sandals in Paris and on *Ile de Ré* but on the farm, for obvious reasons, we wore custom made, hob nailed shoes. The cobbler drew the outline of my feet on a heavy brown paper to use as a pattern to cut out the wooden sole. He carved the heels, then nailed the leather high tops to the sides of the soles. He then punched the holes for laces, and hammered octagonal hobnails in the soles, to keep the wood from wearing as rapidly. I had blisters on both feet until the leather softened.

Serge came to visit again for a week during summer vacation but we didn't spend much time together; he was too busy meeting girls his age or older. I could see why.

One of my duties that summer, was to go to the manure pile, combine some of that pungent mixture with straw, flatten it out and cut it into square cakes, to dry in the sun. When dry, I stacked them on a wheelbarrow to transport them to a covered storage shed. These "cakes" would supplement our coal supply for the winter.

Soon after Serge's departure we began to hear bombing in the distance. Not often yet, but much more frequently than we had in the past.

One August morning, we heard not only bombing, but what the old World War I soldiers called artillery fire. This went on for a few days. Wave after wave of airplanes, mostly bombers, flew over. From time to time we saw German trucks, full of soldiers going east, instead of to the coast as they normally did. We had lost electricity, so we couldn't listen to the "BBC" for news of the war elsewhere. A German convoy made up of all types of vehicles, even bicycles, went speeding through town. The usual German precision was gone; they were driving chaotically with the single purpose of fleeing from the area.

One of my neighbors and I climbed a tall windmill at his house. We stood for hours on the circular platform at the top, waiting, not knowing exactly what to expect. We didn't even come down to relieve ourselves. Instead we had a contest to see how far out our streams could reach on the bushes beneath us. In the distance, clouds of dust grew, until they were just on the edge of town. Then all seemed to stop. We wanted to go see what was going on, but we were forbidden.

A little later a different looking convoy came into town. There were soldiers in and on trucks and tanks. The **AMERICANS** had arrived to liberate us and all of France. Pandemonium broke out. French, American and English flags appeared from hiding, welcoming the soldiers, who waved their arms and helmets in return. All physically able villagers rushed from their homes, into the street. The convoy had to come to a halt, to keep from running over the worshiping throng. Countless bottles of wine were brought to our liberators. They were intended to be gifts, but for each bottle the GI's would give tinned rations, chocolate bars and chewing gum in return.

My classmates and I walked around admiring and touching tanks; trucks and machine gun mounted Jeeps. All had the famous white stars painted within a circle, on hoods and doors. I looked at one tank for a long time. The iron monster seemed to be softened by a straw broom attached to the opened gun turret, sticking up like a personal flag.

One of the soldiers seemed to take pity on me, and lifted me up on his tank. I scrambled scraping my knees, until I could look in from the open turret hatch. I was accustomed to barnyard smells, and of fermenting wine. But the odor of fuel, sweat and urine mixed, hanging heavy in this metal vault was overwhelming. I didn't understand how these men could stay in those large metal canisters for weeks at a time. Even though, I realized that they were sacrificing their comforts and sometimes their very lives, for us to be free. I was thankful and I was glad.

Though I was the kid who didn't cry at funerals, I had tears in my eyes, I didn't know why. I felt that maybe now my father would return from the concentration camp. The soldier who had lifted me up, saw the tears before I could wipe them. He went down into the tank and came out with a chocolate bar, and a whole pack of chewing gum, just for me. I put the chocolate bar in my pocket to share with Amie later. But I sat down on the gun turret to peel the package of chewing gum. He sat next to me, pulled out a small bible from his shirt pocket, opened it, and showed me a photograph of his wife and a young boy, about my age. He stared at it for a long time then put his arm around my shoulders, gave me a squeeze and jumped down to the ground. He helped me down from the tank, and sent me on my way. Before I turned around to run to the next truck in line, I saw the tears in his eyes.

The Americans stayed in town that night. The French almost fought with each other, for the privilege of hosting at least one G.I. in their home. They were given food and wine, enough to take back to those few that remained to guard the convoy. Several stayed at our house, not only for a cooked meal and wine, but also for baths and a clean bed. They even slept two to a bed. They were so tall! Amazingly, though they didn't speak French, and we spoke no English, we communicated very well with hand signals, wide gesticulation, loud enunciation and a lot of smiles. It seemed that if one couldn't speak the other's language, voicing words more slowly, and in a louder tone, should certainly make the other understand much better.

Late that night I went to bed thinking that surely the war was going to be over, and again that my father would certainly be coming home from the concentration camp. I worried bout him trying to find us. Since we were not in Paris, he would surely know to go to La Flotte, there we would eventually be re-united. I was so excited that I couldn't sleep thinking about it. Eventually I did doze off, and later was awakened by the roar of engines. I threw on my clothes and ran into the street to get my last glimpse of our liberators.

The GI's were preparing the trucks and tanks for the next leg of their trip. The ones in front of our house, filled cans with water from our well. Others filled a tank wagon from a house further down the street. They made up a bucket brigade, passing buckets from man to man. Earlier the priest had walked down the entire line, blessing each vehicle with holy water. We all waved goodbye, calling after them, "*Bonne chance et merci, merci, mille fois merci*". (Good luck and thank you, thank you, a thousand times thank you)

It was not over. The bombing continued. Seldom close to us, unless a bomber was hit by anti aircraft fire on the way to his target. Then he would jettison his load in our fields to limp back to England. Often we heard the rumble in the distance. At first we called it thunder but it sounded more like children playing on kettledrums.

A few days later a ragged group of Frenchmen came to town. They arrived driving delivery trucks and riding motorcycles and even bicycles. The only uniform they wore was the black beret and the blue, white and red *brassard,* (armband) with the ever present Lorraine Cross, identifying them as members of the FFI. They tried to requisition any motorized vehicle they could find. Their mission was to help the Allies root out the remaining pockets of Germans. The residents of Siecq would have been willing to help but the Germans had already confiscated anything that had wheels.

The FFI were also the source of underground communications. They told us that "le General de Gaule and the FFI had liberated Paris on the 25th of August". We were now able to receive news updates from other areas.

The older brother of one of my schoolmates from Ile de Ré was in one of the groups. What excitement! We were able to receive recent news of La Flotte. *Ile de Ré* was within a large crescent from Nantes to Bordeaux that was still occupied. The island was virtually isolated. It had been a significant fortification that the Germans did not want to surrender. I wondered if I would ever see Serge or my mother again? We had not heard from them in several weeks.

A few days after the news, I was in the courtyard raking the gravel paths, when through the dust I had raised, I saw an apparition. It was Serge riding through the large open wooden gate. He came right up to me grinned and spoke. "Here we are!" He tried to lean his bicycle against a post but it fell to the ground, almost taking him with it. I shook my head rubbed the dust out of my eyes with my wrist but he was still there. I looked past him. Maman had leaned her bicycle against the gate, and was half running half stumbling toward me, calling to me through sobs of joy and exhaustion. I grabbed Serge's hand and pulled him with me toward her. We almost collided and as a trio we embraced. Maman was really crying now and so was Serge. I came close, but at first I held back my tears, then I also wept, tears flowing silently down my cheeks.

Amie met us at the door; she was coming to check on the commotion. Maman tried to smile and went upstairs; we didn't see her again until the next day. Serge on the other hand went to the kitchen with Amie and me. She prepared him a snack of rabbit paté and bread, along with a glass of undiluted red wine. His hunger somewhat satisfied, he started to recount the story of the previous few months since he had left Siecq.

Chapter Ten

Their daily routine was pretty much the same as when I had been in La Flotte. Serge attended school when he was not working on the farm. The food was even scarcer, and the electricity had been turned off, for the civilian population. Most of the remaining residents were the elderly, who, like Pepére had refused to leave earlier. There was little fuel for lamps and the few candles remaining were hoarded in case of serious illness. So everyone went to bed at dark.

Serge talked to maman about the boredom they felt. Very few things were happening on *Ile de Ré*, only the frequent bombing raids continued. The Germans seldom sent up fighters to engage the allied airplanes flying directly over them. Anti-aircraft fire from the ground continued but it didn't seem quite as intense as it had been in the previous months. The German soldiers never smiled anymore. They all looked tired; many of them even looked like they went several days without shaving. This was something that was never allowed before.

The frustration of not having any news of the outside was starting to tell on Maman. She and Serge, though weary with the times, were still always energetic and impatient. They needed to leave the Island. They had heard nothing from me in several months. Maman had told me not to write since she feared that my letters would allow the authorities to find me. Maman decided she and Serge would leave the island and come to Siecq to be close to me.

Serge told Maman that, "To try to leave the island now is too dangerous. It means we would be shot if we were caught." He reminded her that the town crier had come just a few days before, announcing that French civilians could no longer obtain passes to go to the mainland. Only German soldiers would be allowed to take the ferry, then solely with military orders. Even senior officers who had been allowed to travel at will were restricted to their posts.

Maman, generally positive, responded "At a time like this nothing is impossible, I will show you that if you are determined you can accomplish the impossible."
That decision made, Maman went to the German Headquarters in La Flotte and officially requested a pass to the mainland. Of course the request was denied. She then requested the pass for health reasons, from the French clerk in city hall. He denied her request, but told her that there was one final option available to her. She could obtain a doctor's certificate, countersigned, and stamped by the mayor.

Maman pedaled her bicycle to St. Martin to the new family doctor, then convinced him to issue her a certificate of failing health. Within a few hours, she presented the certificate to the mayor's secretary who told her that the mayor was out, and would not be back for a few days. Maman knew very well that he was there, but she also felt that he did not want to take the responsibility of signing such a contestable document.

Maman, all of five feet two inches, stepped back to look into the secretary's eyes and told him " Well then you, Monsieur, must issue the pass." He was quick to remind her that it was against the regulations, and no one was to be allowed to leave the island. She looked up at him again reminding him that he was a Frenchman, and that he should do his utmost to help another Frenchman. And while he was at it, he should make out a pass for Serge. Reluctantly he agreed, reminding her that it was extremely dangerous to be traveling during these times. " I know that it is dangerous for me and my son, but I am willing to take the risk, therefore you should be willing to allow me the opportunity."

She had conquered this half of the challenge. With the passes in hand, she went back to German headquarters, where she presented the doctor's certificate and the French passes to the officer in charge. Using her best conversational German, Maman told the officer that it was imperative that she return to the mainland to see a specialist. He looked at the papers to make sure that they were in order, then took the opportunity to ask her if Serge was her only child. Taken by surprise, she hesitated briefly, but quickly came back with a, "No, I have a younger son in a colony". He looked down at her, then placed his stamp on the documents. Maman turned to leave; he wished her a "good, safe, trip and a lot of luck". She took it to mean "Lady, you will be lucky if you make it alive".

Maman jumped off her bicycle calling for Serge to pack. He met her at the door. She waved the passes in front of him saying, "You see, nothing is impossible and don't ever give up!" They went upstairs, to pack. Maman remembered a line in one of my father's smuggled letters, "Never let them go away from you when they need you..."

That night was sad. Pepére and Mamie both thought that they would never see maman and Serge again. They all felt pretty much the same way. In spite of that they went to bed early. The drone of bombers passing overhead to wreak havoc with our oppressors in the east broke the silence of the night, waking Serge. He was restless and slept very little until the dawn.

Early that morning maman and Serge mounted their bicycles. A small valise, holding the bare essentials for each, was tied to the back fenders. They rode to Sablanceaux and boarded the ferry. They were the only civilians on board, and were surveyed very suspiciously by the young German and Italian troops, who were leaving the island, headed for the front.

The passage seemed to take forever. Maman was becoming very nervous, fearing that the soldiers would detain them when they reached port in La Palice. She tried to make the time pass by surveying each soldier and his equipment. During that exercise, she realized how poorly equipped the soldiers were, compared to the way that they had been a few months before. Only about half had gas masks and their boots were very worn. It looked to her that the Germans must really be in trouble.

The ferry captain took three tries, to dock the boat. During that process Maman told Serge to get ready to disembark as soon as the gangplank was lowered. Again, they mounted their bicycles and pedaled off the boat going straight to La Rochelle. Once there, they had to find the road to Angoulême. La Rochelle to Siecq was just too far to reach this late in the day. The crossing had taken much longer than usual. They would have to spend the night and leave the next day.

Maman and Serge were now on a side street, clear of the area that the German garrison generally used. They took their time finding the house of Mamie's friends with hopes of spending the night.

The lady and her son appeared very happy to receive news of *Ile de Ré*. They also, had been without electricity for several weeks.

The son was only two years older than Serge, but said proudly that he was very active with the F.F.I. and was seldom home. He was pleased to give the report that the allies had attempted to invade France, but sad, because they had failed. Of course by now that attempt was common knowledge. The Germans were really not trying to suppress the news of a victory of sorts.

The four of them had been talking for some time, when an explosion outside broke the silence. Serge ran to the door and as he opened it young man of eighteen years or so almost knocked him down, running into the house screaming, "hide me, hide me!" Serge's new friend without thinking told the intruder to "go upstairs". A young neighbor girl came in at the same time. She said that it could not have been a real bomb, so it had to be either a grenade or a home made bomb. In any case she was scared and did not want to stay home by herself.

All five now looked at each other wondering who the boy was, and what he may have done. The young intruder had been dressed in blue pants and white shirt, as most of the older students dressed during that time. The owner of the house was first to speak, exclaiming that they were "stupid" for taking in a stranger who must certainly be running from either the police or the Germans. In either case, they could all be in danger for helping a fugitive. Her son looked at her saying, "He is a Frenchman who needs help. If I were the one running in someone else's house, would you not want them to help me? Anyway, it's the end of the subject, he is here now, so it is too late."

Serge had been listening; that in itself was unusual. Serge generally did the talking. The moment of silence, always present after a declarative sentence, was ripped by the sound of machine gun fire coming ever closer. Serge sprang into action. He found a deck of cards and sat at the kitchen table. Quickly, he dealt them as he told the others to join him. They would pretend to be playing a game. They all felt that soon there would be a search of the neighborhood. Almost at that instant a rifle butt pounded the door, making them all jump in fear.

Again Serge jumped up opened the door, and in near perfect German said, "Yes! What do you want?" The three Germans in the doorway looked at him slightly amused at the aggressiveness of this small fourteen-year-old. Still they were serious about the reason for being there. "We are looking for a man in a white shirt and blue pants". Serge happened to be wearing the same combination. He looked down at himself and said, "It could be me!" Again they smiled and said "No! You are too small, but we have to search the house. He has not had the time to get far."

They searched at will. There was no stopping them without attracting attention. Serge tagged along with them, exchanging pleasantries, and even telling jokes in German. The search revealed nothing and they seemed satisfied. As they were turning to leave one of the soldiers spotted the stairway. He hesitated, poised to leave, then seemed to change his mind. "I am sure that there is no one there but duty commands that I go upstairs to look."

The five of them froze. Abject fear materialized instantly in the room. Even Serge, who had appeared lighthearted throughout the search, now became quiet. He caught himself, thinking that if he changed his attitude, surely they would become suspicious. Two soldiers climbed the stairs carelessly; the sound of jackboots and a swinging shoulder slung rifle occasionally hitting the wall breaking the now heavy silence. Serge went along with them, unsure of what he could or would do, when they found the refugee.

As he expected, the soldiers found the fugitive lying on top of the bed, a grimace of sheer terror distorted his face. The soldiers had been so sure that no one would be there, that they were not prepared for him. They scrambled, bringing their rifles around to the ready, yelling at the boy to be still. Fear and uncertainty brings on either uncontrolled shouting or utter silence. They chose shouting, one louder than the other. Hearing the commotion, the third soldier sprang up the stairs two at the time.

Serge tried to be heard. "We were playing cards and he developed a headache, so Maman told him to go up and lie down in the dark. Anyway, many people dress the same way, he can't be the one you are looking for." They looked down at Serge and said, "That's enough from you, both of you come downstairs, *schnell*."

They chose the kitchen as the interrogation room. One of the soldiers noted that there had only been five chairs around the card table, not six. He started by asking simple question, name, age and then finally for papers. The boy was so petrified that he could not even manage to give his name. The more questions were asked of him, the more withdrawn he became. The Germans took his fear to be lack of cooperation, so they ordered both he and Serge to follow them outside. Maman realized that if the boys left the house they would never return. They would probably be sent to a concentration camp, or worse! If the police did find out that the boy threw the grenade that killed two Germans, he would undoubtedly be shot. Serge would surely be next for attempting to help, and to hide him.

Maman tried to intervene in French but they would not even listen to her. Her knowledge of German had worked for her before, so maman took a deep breath and tried again, this time in their tongue. "My son is only fourteen years old, he is just a boy and could not have been involved in this matter but if you must take him, take me also!" That exclamation took them back a little. They were accustomed to loud impassioned supplications, accompanied by tears. Maman was familiar enough with the methods of the German police, to know that she must do something different. She had to gain their respect. Throughout history victors have always taken advantage of the vanquished, particularly if they are meek.

The resistance from that small woman took them by surprise, and threw off their sense of procedure. They knew that she had nothing to do with the grenade, and didn't want to get her involved. They felt sure that if she went with them, she also would probably never return.

Forgetting for a moment that both Serge and maman understood German, they carried on a conversation between themselves. Two of them had wives and children and really didn't want to take her son away from her, and certainly didn't want to be responsible for an innocent woman's death. They decided that one of them would go find an officer to make the decision. The other two rounded up all six in the house and had them stand in the garden until the officer came.

The young officer immediately took charge. He pulled his pistol, pointed it at Serge's head as another held a square flash light in his face. The weak beam did little to intimidate him, but the black Luger worked. They interrogated him for a long while. He answered in controlled German seemingly unruffled. Next maman had to endure the same treatment. She also replied in German, perhaps a little too haughtily. They told her that she was in a very precarious and dangerous position, and to only answer the questions. She did add that she didn't think the boy could have done anything. They looked at the hostess's son, asked his name and who he was and went on to the neighbor girl then the mother. Serge again became the interpreter.

Their decision made, they took the young man away. Uncontrolled sobs and a flood of tears were visible on the young man's cheeks, as he struggled in their grasp while being escorted from the house at gunpoint. He stumbled in fear, and to add to his dilemma, a large wet spot grew down his left pant leg. The officer told maman and Serge that they were to stay available, as they were to be witnesses. A wave of helplessness came over the ones who remained. They were incapable of doing anything to save the strange boy. There was very little conversation, the hostess was very upset that her house had been compromised by such an unfortunate event. She knew that her house would now be under surveillance; but she did allow maman and Serge to remain the rest of the night.

Almost immediately they went upstairs to the room that the nameless young man had adopted. They climbed in the same bed fully dressed and began to discuss their course of action.

Surely if they remained they would be detained for an undetermined period of time. There was one thing in their favor, during the interrogation the Germans must have assumed that they belonged in the house since they didn't ask for their destination. Maman and Serge stayed awake all night, first making plans and then changing them, time and again. Their final decision was to leave early, at the same time that the citizens of La Rochelle would be leaving for work. Any earlier and they would draw attention to themselves.

It was a good thing that they had not planned on sleeping. The Germans walked up and down the streets all night, occasionally shooting guns, to keep the citizens in fear of them. Full of apprehension, they rose when the town awoke. Soon bicycles and pedestrians appeared hesitantly on the street. Maman decided that they absolutely had to leave. "We can stay here, not sure of what will happen, but we know that it won't be good. In spite of what we said last night, I am pretty sure the boy threw the grenade and the Germans must also know. If we go and are caught it won't be any worse than staying. We absolutely must go. There is only one chance, it is now, so we must take it."

They got up, thanked their hostess and walked out of the garden gate pushing their bicycles. Prudence dictated that they leave their valises behind. They had filled their pockets with the bare necessities and maman's valuables and whatever else they could secure to their bodies. Their hostess had not offered them any food for their journey. So they hoped to find something to eat on the way.

They were concerned for their hostess. Surely the Germans would go to her house to look for them. She told maman that she didn't want to know where they were going. That way she could truthfully say, that she did not know.

Maman had decided that in order to get as far as possible as quickly as they could; they must take the train. They pushed and rode their bicycles to the station. There were no trains, and no one could tell them when there would be another. The last one had left three days before.

The choice was made for them; they had to ride their bicycles the next hundred kilometers to Siecq.

Chapter Eleven

The ancient city gates had been set up as checkpoints for all travelers. Papers had to be in order and passes had to be approved by the French police; then countersigned by the local German command.

Maman and Serge felt that their names had not yet been given to all the gates to be detained, so they would take the chance. The Germans relied on fear of the population to control road movements, so the gate guards were usually veterans of World War I, not the fervent devotees to Hitler's cause, which one might expect.

Maman held out the letter and telegram that Doctor Metzger had procured for her to come see me in La Flotte. One of the two guards inspected the papers, while Serge made small talk with the other, who appeared to be old enough to be his grandfather. Serge spoke of his trips to Hungary, and of the beauty of the German countryside, as they had traveled through it.

The inspector asked a few questions, probably because he was expected to; and then handed the papers to his cohort who was still talking about his family. They did point out the old date on the letter. Maman said that I was still ill and that they had to go to me. The two guards conferred momentarily thinking that this woman and child could not offer any hazard to the "Third Reich". They smiled and told them to pass.

Though they had put up a good front during the gate examination, they were both scared that something would go wrong. Maman whispered to Serge, "smile and wave". They smiled as they pushed their bicycles past the gate, mounted and pedaled, increasing their speed to get out of sight as quickly as possible. Serge's heart was pounding so hard he thought passers by could hear it. They traveled all day, with only a couple of rest stops in the woods.

The voyage was going well, though they were exhausted and hungry. A river appeared to the right, winding through the woods in the distance. They thought that it was the one that flowed through St. Jean D'Angely. At dusk, they had to make the decision to either go into town to stay in a hotel, for perhaps a good night's sleep, or to hide in some dense woods before reaching town. Maman said that it was going to be a nice night. She decided that they should not take a chance of having to leave the city through the guard gate in the morning. This time, they might not be as successful as they had been in La Rochelle. They left the road and found an inviting bed under a great oak.

Serge on his hands and knees, raked a few leaves to use as a pillow for each of them. That was the extent of their preparation for bed. They lay down and were asleep at once.

Daylight came too soon. They got up, went to the riverbank to wash the sleep from their eyes. Next they started looking for food. The best they could do was a few bunches of grapes and an apple tree. They each filled their pockets with apples for later in the day. As they sat on a fallen tree to eat, Serge spoke of the young man who was taken away by the Germans two days before. Was he even still alive? He wondered out loud.

This thought set the mood for the morning. Serge, though usually gregarious and even interesting, was distressed about his lack of pals. New friendships were almost non existent. You didn't dare get close to anyone. First you didn't know if you could trust them or they you; then personal encounters were now so short, you never knew how quickly you would be separated, sometimes even by death. It seemed not to be worth taking a chance on cultivating a friendship.

They had to get underway; they still had over twenty-five kilometers to go if they rode through St. Jean D'Angely. They had to make the decision to either travel several kilometers out of their way or to go through the middle of town. Fear of capture led them along a river path. They would have to find a way to cross the river *Boutton.* The further they traveled up the path, the closer to town they were getting. The path was now running parallel to the main road, just a couple hundred meters away.

The sound of gunfire interrupted their thinking. At first, it seemed to be fairly distant, but as the shooting continued, it became sharper and closer. It had to be the underground chasing the Germans in a skirmish. Maman told Serge to get off his bicycle.They would hide in a clump of trees until the shooting was over. The ground around them was littered with the remains of an earlier engagement. Remnants of clothing and brass shell casings were scattered all around, even a burned out car was still smoldering in the middle of a field.

They could see smoke through the trees in the distance. A house had been set on fire; presumably to flush out the fighters. There was no way of knowing which group had been in the house. The gunfire ceased almost as quickly as it had begun. They waited a few minutes to be sure that it would not start again, then they went on. The path now joined the main road. They mounted their bicycles, constantly looking from side to side, and over their shoulders. They passed a few more burning houses as they came to the outskirts of the town. The closer to town they rode, the more apprehensive maman became. They were so busy looking around and behind them, that they really didn't pay attention to the town's buildings in front of them.

Serge, riding ahead, looked up and yelled at maman; "We are free, we are free!" She looked at him in exasperation, thinking that he must really be tired. She was going to chastise him for yelling and drawing attention to them. She looked up ahead, and saw the Stars and Stripes of the United States of America, flying on the church spire. A little further they saw the English flag, then the blue, white and red French tricolor. There was even a Russian flag.

It had to be "*La Liberation*!"

Maman stopped her bicycle, let it fall to the ground and knelt in prayer of thanksgiving. She wept, she had not cried in the presence of anyone for months. Now, whether the tears were of joy, sorrow, relief or even frustration she did not know. She had demonstrated a lot of strength and courage out of necessity, but now she simply could not hold back the tears.

Serge on the other hand, always dramatic; stood at attention by the side of the road and sang the "Marseillaise". The Germans had forbidden the playing or singing of the French anthem or of any patriotic French songs. Now he would make up for it, because France was free!

They walked and rode their bicycles into town, looking for the rail station. Fifteen minutes after finding it they were aboard an electric train on the way to Siecq. Providence seemed to have been on their side for this entire trip. The train had been waiting to leave. They had just enough time to buy their tickets and board. They were even allowed to bring their bicycles, providing they left them in the corridor of the car.

The train was packed with civilians, seemingly going nowhere. They had been restricted for so long, that now they were traveling solely for the sake of going. No one was sitting; they milled from one compartment to the next, exchanging pleasantries and telling stories of privation and fear. They sang and they cried, but joy by far outweighed their sadness.

The two hours flew by. The buildings in Siecq also were festooned with dozens of allied flags. Maman and Serge walked their bicycles through the village, savoring the look of joy and relief, on all they encountered.

Recent events had been going too well, maman thought that through the happiness of the people, there had to be a disaster. I was hurt, gone, or worse yet I had been killed during the fighting. She asked a woman passing by, if the fighting had been fierce in and around Siecq. Her reply was "Almost not at all, the Nazis went speeding through here with their tails between their legs, and the Americans followed just a few hours behind".

His story told; Serge went up to his room and slept the "sleep of the dead", Mamie called it.

The next morning at breakfast, we spoke of Mamie and Pepére, of La Flotte and the fact that we were totally cut off from them. Maman worried about them constantly, and we missed them a lot. They probably did not know that this part of France at least, was no longer occupied. We received general news by the underground about *Ile de Ré*.

Times there, had been hard earlier, but now they were really difficult. Food and clothing seemed to be a luxurious dream of the past. More Germans had assembled on the island feeling safer there, since it was one of their better fortifications. Their supply lines no longer open, they joined the French in knowing what hunger was. They searched for food every where. They were forced to send foraging parties out to the mainland to the "free" zone. They disguised themselves in civilian clothes. We heard the FFI even caught two dressed in nun's habits, then shot them as spies.

Pepere and Mamie were a little more fortunate than other villagers. They owned three gardens, two of which were surrounded by tall stone walls, the top guarded by broken bottle bases imbedded in mortar. Pepére had been able to grow basic crops, potatoes, carrots and such without being under the eyes of passing soldiers.

His friend *Claudomire*, was the local butcher who always seemed to be able to find a pig to dress. They swapped pork for vegetables. Then the two of them shared their bounty with two other couples with whom they had played cards for decades. The subterfuge they underwent, to transport the food had become a real game to them. They disguised the packages as gifts; they placed them in buckets covered with coal; and whatever other ingenious plans they could devise. Either they were pretty good at it or all the other villagers just didn't care what they were doing. In any case, they were never caught.

Maman had applied for a pass to go back to Paris. She was concerned about the three Jewish ladies she had hidden in our apartment on *Rue de la Tourelle*. She had not heard from them in over a year. She thought it strange, since she had given them a home, after their husbands had also been arrested and imprisoned.

Authorized travel for civilians was still almost impossible. The Germans were no longer in charge but the French police, the military and the FFI had almost complete control. They were absorbed in capturing German deserters, trying to make their way back to Germany in civilian clothes. Her travel permit was denied!

Even if approved, it would have been almost impossible for her to travel; railroads had been bombed, roads also had huge craters in them, and bridges had been demolished. Even if she had been strong enough to travel by bicycle, it was really taunting danger, if not asking for possible death.

Maman became ill, she was unable to work in the fields so she wrote letters that were never mailed. She wrote to almost everyone she had ever known in the morning, then in the evening she would tear the letters neatly in four, and burn them in the stove. She took short walks, constantly thinking that she was wasting time there. She was with her two boys, but she needed to go to see if by some miracle, my father had been released. If so, he would have absolutely no way of finding us.

Toward the end of November 1944 roads had been repaired sufficiently to allow restricted travel. Maman had begun to regain some strength. She went around Siecq trying to find a way, anywhere north, by any means. She heard that a French soldier was going to Niort. He was to drive a truck to the headquarters of the French military police. That was only seventy kilometers north, still, it was better than sitting where she was, so she convinced him to let her ride with him.

She arrived at the headquarters and requested a pass to go to Paris. She thought it to be a simple request, and a decision could be made in a few minutes. She showed the officer her papers, explained her situation and answered questions for hours. During their conversation, the officers learned that maman spoke several languages, including German. They wanted to enlist her help in finding German deserters.

German collaborators and sympathizers, were being identified and punished. They were not shot or imprisoned unless their collaboration caused the death of a Frenchman. They were humiliated, particularly the women whose heads were shaved in public.

Maman wanted to do her duty, but she was still ill and weak; she felt that she really could not be of help at this time. She assured them that if they would issue her a pass to Paris, she would return and spend time with the FFI, when she regained her strength. They agreed to those terms, and issued the pass. She managed to find a ride in a military car going south to Bordeaux, from there she would be able to find a train to Paris. That line had been repaired.

Serge and I stayed in Siecq. Earlier we had made the harvest. The grape crop was not that good. Many of the grapevines had suffered significant damage from the cold during the previous winter. But the new wine promised to be very good.

Coal was still hard to find. Winter was almost at hand. Fortunately I had made plenty of the dung cakes during the summer. Otherwise, the times were almost back to normal for the local people. They went from farm to farm helping each other gather the grapes. It was six days a week of back breaking work, from dawn to dusk.

Sunday was the day of rest in spite of the need to harvest. Mass was important to all, Serge played the church organ as he had for the last few weeks. The sermon was short. It was one of thanksgiving for the end of the fighting and for the harvest. The vineyards had suffered almost no damage from the war. The mass being over, all that had participated in the "vendange" came to our house. Probably, fifteen to twenty people. The women pitched in to prepare the food while the men sat outside smoking and swapping stories. At lunch, they were all joyful; they laughed, told more stories and didn't seem to worry about having lost members of their families. I could not understand how they did that. It was as if the war had never happened for them.

Not so for me, I still thought of my father and how much I missed him. I wanted him to come back. We had many things to do together. He had said that he would teach me to bind books and to play the violin. I thought of my classmate Jacques, from Paris, who was there one day and not the next. I enjoyed being with the Mechain family, and really liked them and their friends, but it was not the same.

Lunch over, the men adjourned to the garden where they started a game of "boule", gambling on every roll of the ball. Concentration on the shots intensified, while good-humored chiding increased, small sums of money changed hands after each game. When the men tired of the game, the children were allowed to play, but could not gamble.

Serge and I were in a comfortable routine; he had made a few friends closer to his age, and I still had my friends. We didn't do anything with the underground anymore, but we managed to enjoy ourselves.

Father Gyula and Son Guy

Last Photo, Paris, April - 1942

Brother Serge, Mother Louise & Guy
Paris, September - 1941

Serge, Gyula & Guy

Paris, September - 1941

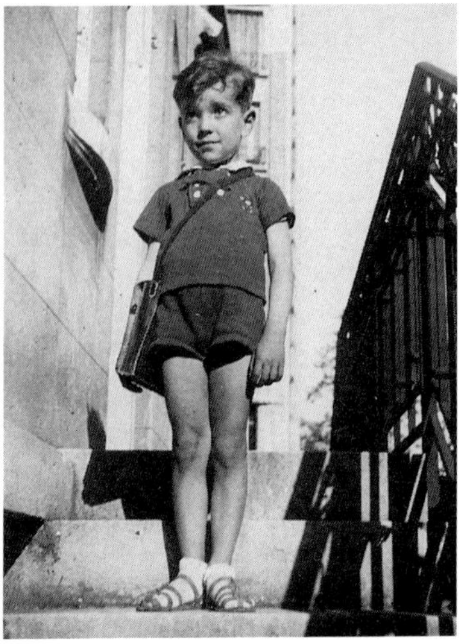

Guy

Paris, September - 1941

Guy
Paris, June - 1942
with school bag his Father made

Guy , La Flotte, Ile De Ré, 1943 in Grandfather's garden before going to Siecq. Note inverted wine bottle borders.

Gyula Geller, June - 1929
His press identification for
the UJSAG daily

Part of the group prior to their
arrest on October 13, 1942.
Gyula Geller in center

Family in Hungary, 1935, before the birth of Guy, Serge is in the middle.

Uncle Karoly, Guy's namesake, and his father's sister, Anne

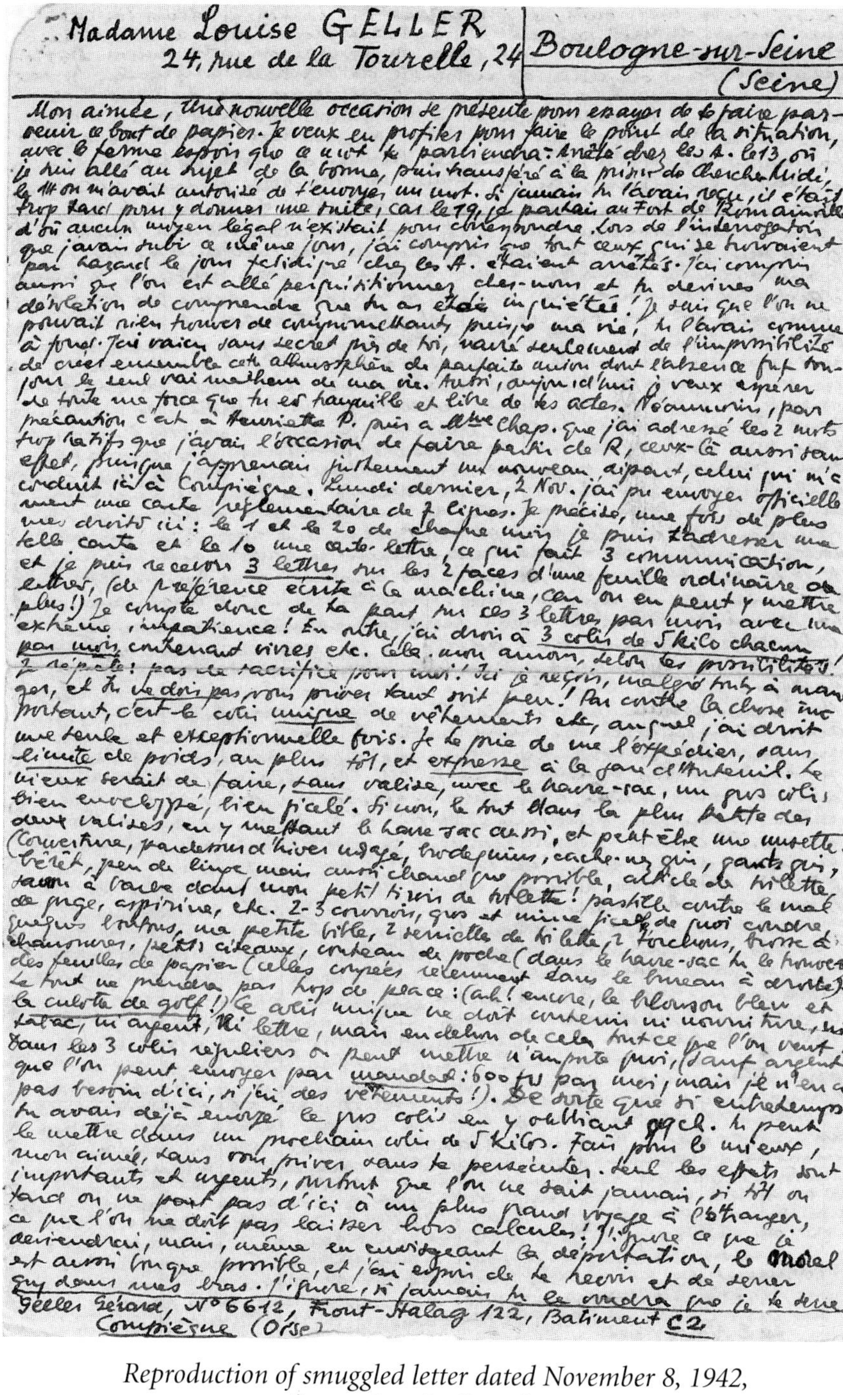

Madame Louise GELLER
24, rue de la Tourelle, 24
Boulogne-sur-Seine
(Seine)

Mon aimée, une nouvelle occasion se présente pour essayer de te faire parvenir ce bout de papier. Je veux en profiter pour faire le point de la situation, avec le ferme espoir que ce mot te parviendra: Arrêté chez les A. le 13, où je suis allé au sujet de la bonne, puis transféré à la prison du Cherche-Midi, le 14 on m'avait autorisé de t'envoyer un mot. Si jamais tu l'avais reçu, il était trop tard pour y donner une suite, car le 19, je partais au Fort de Romainville, d'où aucun moyen légal n'existait pour correspondre. Lors de l'interrogatoire que j'avais subi ce même jour, j'ai compris que tous ceux qui se trouvaient par hasard le jour fatidique chez les A. étaient arrêtés. J'ai compris aussi que l'on est allé perquisitionner chez nous et tu devines ma désolation de comprendre que tu as été inquiétée! Je sais que l'on ne pouvait rien trouver de compromettant puisque ma vie, tu l'avais comme à jour. J'ai vécu sans secret près de toi, navré seulement de l'impossibilité de créer ensemble cette atmosphère de parfaite union dont l'absence fut toujours le seul vrai malheur de ma vie. Aussi, aujourd'hui je veux espérer de toute ma force que tu es tranquille et libre de tes actes. Néanmoins, par précaution c'est à Henriette P. puis à Mme Chap. que j'ai adressé les 2 mots furtifs que j'avais l'occasion de faire partir de R, ceux-là aussi sans effet, puisque j'apprenais justement un nouveau départ, celui qui m'a conduit ici à Compiègne. Lundi dernier, 2 Nov. j'ai pu envoyer officiellement une carte réglementaire de 7 lignes. Je précise, une fois de plus mes droits ici: le 1 et le 20 de chaque mois je puis t'adresser une telle carte et le 10 une carte-lettre, ce qui fait 3 communications, et je puis recevoir 3 lettres sur les 2 faces d'une feuille ordinaire de lettres, (de préférence écrite à la machine, car on en peut y mettre plus!) Je compte donc de ta part sur ces 3 lettres par mois avec une extrême impatience! En outre, j'ai droit à 3 colis de 5 kilo chacun par mois contenant vivres etc. Cela, mon amour, selon tes possibilités! Je répète: pas de sacrifice pour moi! Ici je reçois, malgré tout, à manger, et tu ne dois pas vous priver tant soit peu! Par contre la chose importante, c'est le colis unique de vêtements etc, auquel j'ai droit une seule et exceptionnelle fois. Je te prie de me l'expédier, sans limite de poids, au plus tôt, et expresse à la gare d'Auteuil. Le mieux serait de faire, sans valise, avec le havre-sac, un gros colis bien enveloppé, bien ficelé. Si non, le tout dans la plus petite des deux valises, en y mettant le havre-sac aussi, et peut-être une musette. (Couverture, pardessus d'hiver usagé, brodequins, cache-nez gris, gants gris, béret, peu de linge mais aussi chaud que possible, article de toilette, savon à barbe dans mon petit tiroir de toilette! pastille contre le mal de gorge, aspirine, etc. 2-3 crayons, gros et mince ficelle de quoi coudre quelques boutons, ma petite bible, 2 serviettes de toilette, 2 torchons, brosse à chaussures, petits ciseaux, couteau de poche (dans le havre-sac tu le trouveras) des feuilles de papier (celles coupées récemment dans le bureau à droite). Le tout ne prendra pas trop de place: (ah! encore, le blouson bleu et la culotte de golf!) Le colis unique ne doit contenir ni nourriture, ni tabac, ni argent, ni lettre, mais en dehors de cela tout ce que l'on veut. Dans les 3 colis réguliers on peut mettre n'importe quoi, (sauf argent que l'on peut envoyer par mandat: 600 frs par mois, mais je n'en ai pas besoin d'ici, si j'ai des vêtements!). De sorte que si entretemps tu avais déjà envoyé le gros colis en y oubliant qqch. tu peux le mettre dans un prochain colis de 5 kilos. Fais pour le mieux, mon aimée, sans vous priver sans te persécuter. Seul les effets sont importants et urgents, surtout que l'on ne sait jamais, si tôt ou tard on ne part pas d'ici à un plus grand voyage à l'étranger, ce que l'on ne doit pas laisser hors calculs! J'ignore ce que je deviendrai, mais, même en envisageant la déportation, le moral est aussi bon que possible, et j'ai espoir de te revoir et de serrer qq dans mes bras. J'espère, si jamais tu le voudra que je te serre

Geller Gérard, No 6612, Front-Stalag 122, Bâtiment C2
Compiègne (Oise)

Reproduction of smuggled letter dated November 8, 1942,
from prison in Compiegne.
Shown at Actual Size

Helen Jacob
Geller
circa 1903
Szentes, Hungary

Ferreol Lucie Celine
Erraudeau
June, 1919
Paris, France

La Flotte, Ile de Ré
aerial view of Harbor taken after
the War - Mid 1950's

Towers at the harbor entrance of La Rochelle,
built 1620's under orders of Cardinal Richelieu.

Mechain Family, April - 1946

left *bottom row* *right*

M. Paul Mechain ***Amie** - Anne Marie Mechain*

Siecq, Building a Hay Stack with Steam Power

Guy, with hat on left

August - 1944

Class Photo, Siecq, 1944-45

Class Photo, Pacific Grove, California, 1946-47

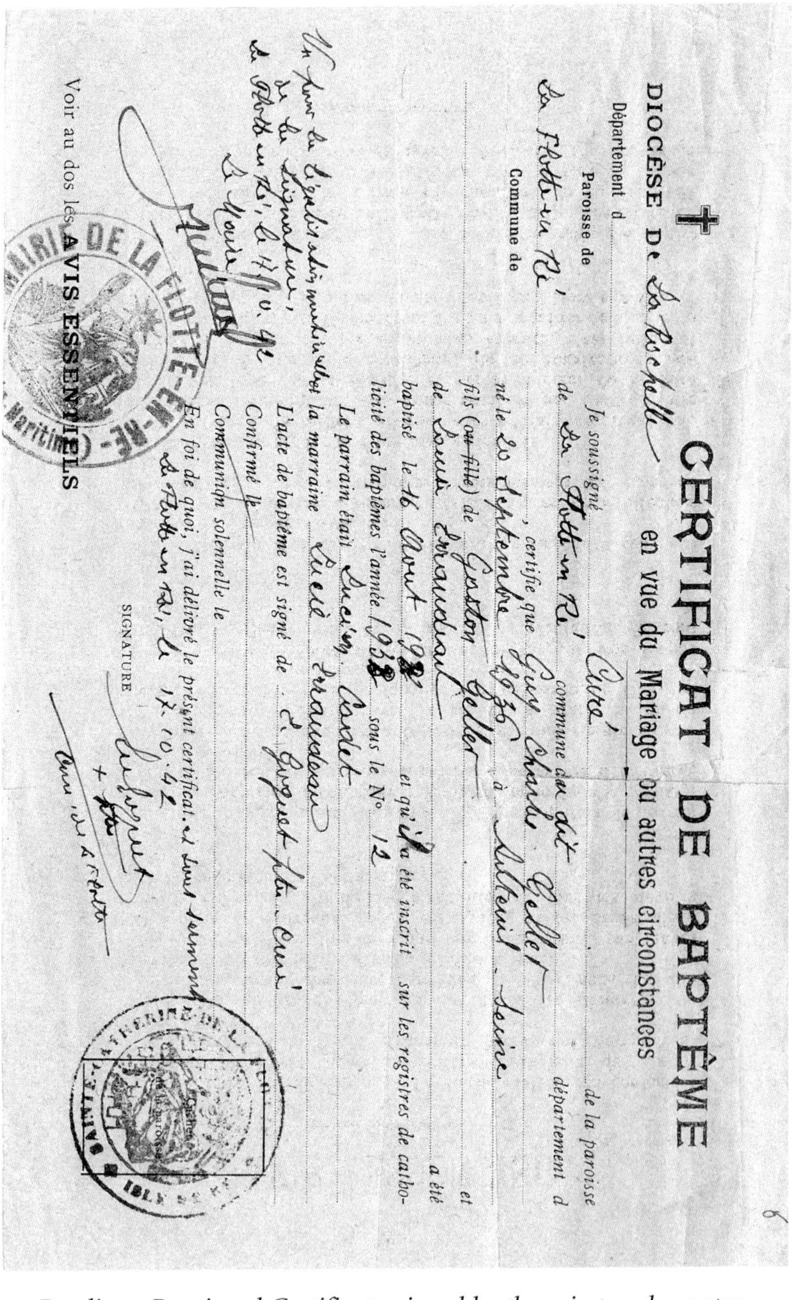

CERTIFICAT DE BAPTÊME

DIOCÈSE De La Rochelle

en vue du Mariage ou autres circonstances

Département d

Paroisse de

La Flotte en Ré

Commune de

Je soussigné Curé de la paroisse de La Flotte en Ré commune du dit département d , certifie que Guy Charles Geller né le 20 Septembre 1936 à Auteuil - Seine fils (~~ou fille~~) de Gaston Geller et de Louise Erraudeau a été baptisé le 16 Aout 1938 et qu'il a été inscrit sur les registres de catholicité des baptêmes l'année 1938 sous le N° 12

Le parrain était Lucien Cardet

la marraine Lucie Erraudeau

L'acte de baptême est signé de E. Guyet ptre. Curé

Confirmé le

Communion solennelle le

En foi de quoi, j'ai délivré le présent certificat.

La Flotte en Ré, le 17.10.42

SIGNATURE

Vu pour la légalisation matérielle de la signature, La Flotte en Ré, le 17.10.42

Le Maire

MAIRIE DE LA FLOTTE-EN-RÉ

Cachet de la paroisse

Voir au dos les **AVIS ESSENTIELS**

Duplicate Baptismal Certificate, signed by the priest and counter-signed by the mayor. Shows Baptism 8-16-38, certificate delivered 10-17-42.

The long way to school after dog bite - Steeple of St. Catherine

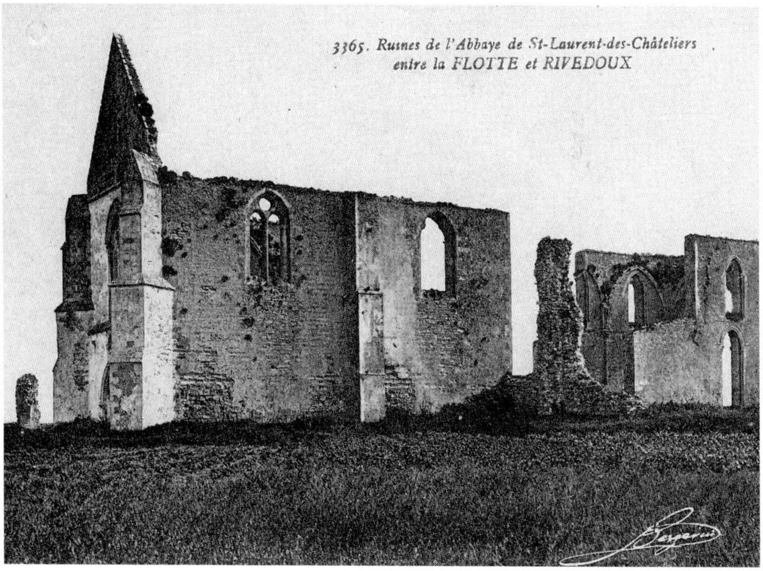

3365. Ruines de l'Abbaye de St-Laurent-des-Châteliers
entre la FLOTTE et RIVEDOUX

Ruins of the "Abbaye de St. Laurent-des-Chateliers,
Re-constructed circa 1468 - Abandoned in 1623 - also known as
"Notre Dame de Ré "

Mother & Guy, 1947
Pebble Beach - 17 Miles Drive
On the middle finger of Guy's left hand is Father's Ring smuggled from prison of Drancy - the day before his departure for Auschwitz.

Mother & Guy at
Club House, Pebble Beach, 1947

Doctor Arthur Russell Moore, Guy & Mary Mitchell Moore
Portland, Oregon, 1948

Guy & Aunt Mitch during Latin lesson,
Pacific Grove, California, 1949

1952, Guy washing milk bottles at Galbraith Dairy, Lancaster, New Hampshire

1952, Wayne & Guy in Lancaster

1953, Shelton, Connecticut
Abraham Levietes, Uncle Abe

1953, Shelton Connecticut,
Best Buddy Bob
One could have FRIENDS in this country.

R.F. SS
Sicherheits-Dienst
Nachrichten-Uebermittlung

XXVC-205

Aufgenommen				Befördert				Raum für Eingangsstempel
Tag	Monat	Jahr	Zeit	Tag	Monat	Jahr	Zeit	
von		durch		an 12 Feb. 1943		durch	15 30	
				Verzögerungsvermerk				
Nr. 7493								

Telegramm — Funkspruch — Fernschreiben — Fernspruch

IV B (IB J alt) BdS
Sa 225a
Rö./Ne.

Paris, den 12. Februar 1943

1. An das
Reichssicherheitshauptamt
- IV B 4 a -
z.Hdn. von SS-Obersturmbann-
führer Eichmann o.V.i.A.

Berlin.

dringend!
sofort vorlegen!

2. An den Inspekteur der Konzentrationslager
Oranienburg

3. An das
Konzentrationslager
Auschwitz/O.S.

Am 11. Februar 1943 um 10,15 Uhr hat der Transportzug 902 den Abgangsbahnhof Le Bourget-Drancy in Richtung Auschwitz mit insgesamt 998 Juden verlassen.

Der erfaßte Personenkreis entspricht den gegebenen Richtlinien.

Transportführer ist Oberleutnant der Ordnungspolizei Kassel, dem die namentliche Transportliste in zweifacher Ausfertigung mitgegeben wurde.

Telex - manifest of Convoy #47 to "Eichmann" in Auschwitz dated February 12, 1943 - describing makeup of convoy. Gyula Gerard Geller, Prisoner # 6612, was immediately marched to the Gas Chamber upon arrival in Auschwitz, February 13, 1943, four months to the day of his arrest.

Chapter Twelve

The postal service was unreliable, so maman, ever resourceful, was able to get letters to us by tipping army truck drivers. There was a troop shuttle from Paris to the La Rochelle area. The entire region across from *Ile de Ré* was being built up. The drivers said that the final action was going to be soon. The Germans could not hold out much longer.

Her letters, usually descriptive and meticulous, were now almost chaotic. Even I, could tell that she was not well. "There was no more coal in Paris, at least not for the general population. Food was as scarce as it had been during the height of the German occupation," she wrote.

She had arrived at the apartment to find it empty. Not only had her hidden tenants disappeared, but so had most of our beautiful furniture. Maman asked the concierge where the ladies were, she replied that she knew nothing of the ladies, nor of the furniture. Maman was disheartened. She felt she should have been furious, but she was simply too weak to work up enough anger to do anything. She had paid such an exorbitant sum, in advance, to that woman for her silence. Not only was she to be quiet about the tenants, but she had agreed as well to care for our apartment. After a few days of searching, maman did find out that the ladies had returned to their homes. They had tried

tried to write, but with no current address, they had mailed letters to *Ile de Ré*. As maman had suspected, the furniture had been there when they left.

Many schools had been demolished, but fortunately only a small part of Serge's had suffered. He returned to his lycée. Sadly, not all his comrades had survived. There were so many empty seats in his class. I was to stay in Siecq until maman sent for me. She was reviving her dream about taking us to America, and her preparations for such a journey were overwhelming.

The FFI had built up a large enough force to attack the Germans on the island. It would be a fierce fight for *Ile de Ré*. Later it was discovered that the island fortifications had been wired to explode at a given command. German pride dictated that an officer should never surrender his command, particularly not to an informal military group of rebels.

The command to start detonating the charges had been given, moments before the French commander entered the German headquarters to negotiate surrender. The French were able to have the command reversed, saving the island shoreline from near total devastation.

We began to hear from maman again during February 1945, but only occasionally. She said that she had been very ill. Her job had been given to someone else, and even with her skills, it was impossible for her to find a new one. She had stayed in the apartment, still with the hope that my father would be coming home. She did not seek out old friends; feeling certain that they also were engrossed in similar family crises. Also, she certainly didn't want to be a burden to anyone.

During the previous two years maman had almost exhausted our funds. Between rent for the apartment in Paris, protection money for the Jewish ladies and bribes to insure my safety, she had spent an enormous sum. Maman soon learned that shopkeepers scorned people like her; those who only had cash.

The economy revolved more around ration coupons, than cash. If you had not moved during the war, obtaining the ration books was no more of a problem than standing in a long line. Each department issued ration books. Coupons were recognized only in the department issued. So, if you had moved, it was a nightmare taking weeks. You needed certification from the home owner in one "department" whose home had been vacated; then one from the owner or concierge of the new home in a different "department", stating that you had moved there permanently. Unscrupulous landlords sometimes extorted large sums, for the privilege of issuing the required certificates. The queues at the markets lasted for hours and seldom yielded satisfying portions, even with the coupons.

The barter system seemed to be most successful. Food, in some areas was the standard of exchange. The butcher took care of the baker. The jeweler got milk for his children. The green grocer exchanged his vegetables for coal and almost no one had butter. Intriguing relationships developed in those months.

For weeks maman stood in lines, and existed solely on meager portions, obtained sometimes only once a week. She became weaker as the days went by. Her constant fighting for two years had weakened her emotionally, to the point of despair. She was tired, physically ill and she stayed cold in the unheated apartment. She went to bed with the intention of remaining there, come what may. The only liquid she drank, was rainwater she caught in a pan on the kitchen windowsill, and a little wine from a few bottles that had been left behind the closet door. The wine had almost turned to vinegar, but it had a little nourishment.

The next two weeks she spent drifting in and out of consciousness, visualizing her younger life. How much fun it had been. She and her parents lived in Paris for a few years. As a young girl she had spent hours with pencil and charcoal, drawing still lives. Then she attended art classes at the Sorbonne, building a foundation for painting in oils. One of her dreams had been satisfied.

She met Harry in one of the bistros close to the University. Harry was a senior officer in the American Red Cross with diplomatic privileges. He overwhelmed her, and soon they were married. Because of her marriage, she became a citizen of the United States of America. She and her new husband traveled all over Europe. They spent one of the most memorable months of her life in Poland, during the summer of 1920. She met and became friends with Paderewski, the pianist/composer who had for a short time been Prime Minister of Poland.

Memories floated to her mind's surface, bringing her thoughts of their Trans-Atlantic voyage, when she met Doctor and Mrs. Moore. He was a research scientist, and she was a Chemistry professor in Oregon. They gave her an open invitation to visit them in California at their summer home. Her wonderful trip to New Orleans flashed before her eyes, then stayed imbedded in her mind for what seemed like days. She would have to return there.

Maman was so weak that she could hardly get up. One midmorning, the sun shone around the closed shutters in her room. She struggled to get up, just long enough to open them, with the hope that there would be enough sun shinning through the glass to warm her. Glancing down into the drive, as she opened one of the steel shutters, she saw three American soldiers throwing oranges to each other in a noisy game of catch. Occasionally they threw an orange to other people who happened to look out of their windows.

Maman pulled back inside and closed the shutters. She was embarrassed at her appearance, and did not want the Americans to think that she was begging for food. She went back to bed for a while. The thought of fresh oranges remained constantly on her mind. How many months, or even years, had it been since she had tasted fresh fruit? A new pang of hunger getting the better of her, she brushed her hair, then went to the kitchen and opened that window. Looking around she saw no one. She gazed across the fence at the estate house, where she and my father had attended formal social functions, the first year they lived in our apartment. Soon after, the Germans had occupied it for their officers' billet. Now the Americans had replaced the Germans.

A GI stepped from behind a wall at the end of our courtyard. Holding out an orange, he asked maman if she would like one. It didn't matter that his French was atrocious, she understood his kind offer. Much to his apparent relief, she replied in English. " My son is returning from vacation tonight, it would be wonderful if I could greet him with an orange." The GI smiled, and threw the orange underhanded. He asked her permission to return later, to bring more oranges after Serge's arrival. Maman told him that he would certainly be welcome, and to bring some friends.

Maman closed the window; remembering the well thought out speech she had prepared for the first American she encountered. It was to have been a speech of welcome, of joy and of appreciation for the hardships, sacrifices and dangers, which he must have encountered in the liberation of France. It certainly had nothing to do with oranges. The only similarity, she mused was that it was in English, the language that she had learned, and had come to love, when she was married to Harry.

Wayne returned late that evening, after Serge's arrival. He was in uniform, wearing an MP's armband. He was a Vermonter, a Yankee, unassuming, somewhat bashful with an air of quiet strength.

He started coming almost daily, bringing whatever rations he could. Maman was convinced that Wayne had saved her from starvation. Occasionally, one or two of his friends joined them. They did odd jobs to stay busy; repairing the plumbing that had frozen and ruptured a few days before. They even managed to repair the gas line for the stove. Wayne took on the cooking of rations he and his friends pooled. That fare brought maman enough nourishment to let her regain a portion of her strength. He gathered a few items, chocolate bars, chewing gum and peanuts so maman could send some of those delicacies to me in Siecq. By the end of March maman had made great strides in regaining her physical strength. More important, she had emerged from the deep despair and depression, that she had allowed to overcome her.

Maman had written a letter home for one of the soldiers. Soon, more came asking her to write to their families, or to read letters from their wives and girl friends. She was amazed, at the number of men who had risked their lives in the fighting for the liberation of France, that were unable to read or write. Others were highly educated but seemed to have very little time for those less able than they.

Trees began sprouting new growth in mid April. Maman left the house for the first time in weeks, guiding a group of soldiers to the Bois de Boulogne, to show them the flowers emerging from a winter's rest. This was the first in a series of outings, where she became the guide to parks, churches and museums.

The eighth of May was an absolutely wonderful day in Paris. The armistice was signed. Normalcy would not return immediately, but now there really was hope.

Chapter Thirteen

Prisoners of all categories and nationalities, liberated from concentration camps by the Allies, were returning to Paris. Stories of the atrocities they had been subjected to went beyond comprehension. Maman could not accept the fact that human beings could sink to the depths of barbarism, necessary to torture and kill fellow men, solely because of the accident of their birth. As she heard more of the accounts from survivors, she became increasingly anxious for my father's welfare.

Maman began a quest of several weeks. She searched in all the offices that dealt with the repatriation of prisoners. She pursued any type of information concerning the life or death of these wretched human beings. She had my father's prisoner number (6612), which had been assigned in the Fort de Romainville the day of his arrest. Making the rounds of offices, she met ex-prisoners who were able to give the authorities first hand information, concerning the known deaths of fellow prisoners whose names they remembered. They felt that they could ease the pain of uncertainty, for the loved ones who were looking for any sign of their fate.

The terrifying names, such as Dachau, Birkenau, Buchenwald and Auschwitz had been mentioned in hushed voices during the Nazi occupation. Now they were being revealed as the fruit of the seeds sown by deranged monsters. Worst fears and beyond, were realized; starvation, torture, savage medical experiments and executions were daily occurrences. The solution for the weak or infirm, had been the gas chamber or a bullet to the head, then the crematorium or a mass grave.

Maman, almost certain that my father had been sent to one of these death camps, prayed that he had been granted the solace of an early death. Still she did not completely give up hope, she began again making inquiries, hoping for new information. There was nothing new. Sadly, she came to the final realization that he would never return.

It was time to make changes in her life. Her decision was to pursue her earlier plan of going to America. That wonderful country she remembered, with the friendly people, would certainly give Serge and me opportunities that we might not have in France.

Maman resumed her contact with the Moores in California. They had corresponded faithfully, during the last twenty years prior to the war. Her last letter to them had been soon after my father's disappearance. She sent a long letter recounting the events of the past three years, explaining our present plight and her solution to resolve that plight. She asked if there might be an opportunity for a job for her where they lived. They replied quickly, with an invitation for the three of us to join them. The red tape would take several months on each side of the Atlantic, so they needed to start right away, if she was really serious about such a move. She began applying for all the necessary papers.

During her ongoing search for word of my father, maman met a young Jewish student who had managed to stay out of prison by working and hiding with the French underground. He was an intelligent, energetic young man, dedicated to the repatriation of other young Jews who had been students at the universities. Disappointment and disillusionment overshadowed the joy of their return. Unable to find their parents, they had to assume that they were no longer alive. German collaborators, now hypocritically turned staunch French patriots, occupied their family's apartments and homes. Though they had survived tremendous hardships, the students needed help in the simple things. Just coping with their new freedom, was sometimes overwhelming.

Our apartment had been made into a haven for three Jewish ladies during the war, now Maman would let it become a haven again. She would make it a base of support, for these young people. The common problem, was their lack of funds to continue their education. They needed money for tuition, books and food. She realized the best way she could help, was by writing old friends and organizations that could support their effort. She wrote letters to Jewish organizations throughout France, England and the United States. Her requests were met with almost immediate success.

The "Union of Jewish Students" was established. Not that it was easy, but the dedication, the thirst for knowledge and the tenacity these young people demonstrated, made her work all the harder for their success. Money was coming in regularly; within a few short months, several hundred students had resumed their studies in medicine, dentistry and law.

Maman was appointed to be one of the directors. No apparent concern was given to the fact that she was the only Gentile in the organization. The "Union" now had an office in the *Palais Royal*. She spent long days there, then continued them at home, where she usually had a few students studying, or meeting to develop "causes".

One day in December 1945, during a meeting at her apartment, a uniformed Red Cross representative came to her door with a parcel and an envelope. The package contained the clothing that my father had worn on the day of his arrest. Maman now in tears, with trembling hands lifted the flap on the unsealed envelope. The enclosed certificate was the typical, cold, official document.

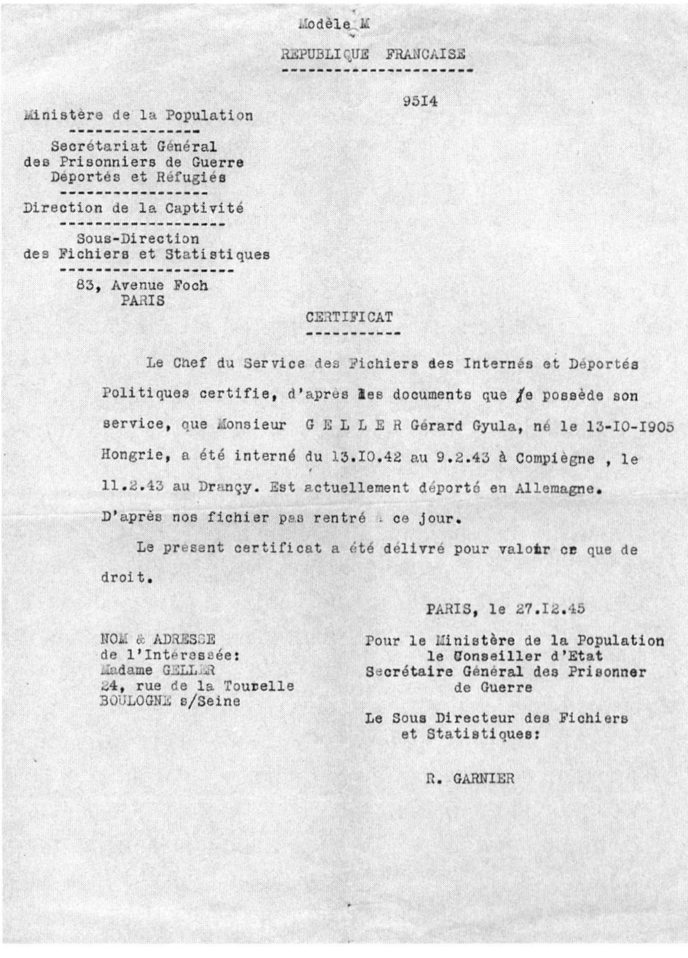

Modèle M

REPUBLIQUE FRANCAISE

9514

Ministère de la Population

Secrétariat Général
des Prisonniers de Guerre
Déportés et Réfugiés

Direction de la Captivité

Sous-Direction
des Fichiers et Statistiques

83, Avenue Foch
PARIS

CERTIFICAT

Le Chef du Service des Fichiers des Internés et Déportés Politiques certifie, d'après les documents que possède son service, que Monsieur G E L L E R Gérard Gyula, né le 13-10-1905 Hongrie, a été interné du 13.10.42 au 9.2.43 à Compiègne , le 11.2.43 au Drançy. Est actuellement déporté en Allemagne. D'après nos fichier pas rentré à ce jour.

Le présent certificat a été délivré pour valoir ce que de droit.

PARIS, le 27.12.45

NOM & ADRESSE
de l'Intéressée:
Madame GELLER
24, rue de la Tourelle
BOULOGNE s/Seine

Pour le Ministère de la Population
le Conseiller d'Etat
Secrétaire Général des Prisonner
de Guerre

Le Sous Directeur des Fichiers
et Statistiques:

R. GARNIER

"The chief of Service of Records for Political Internees and Deportees certifies that according to documents on file in this office, that Monsieur GELLER Gerard Gyula, born 13-10-1905 in Hungary, was interned from October 13, 1942 until February 9, 1943 at Copiegne then to February 11, 1943 at Drancy. Is actually deported to Germany- according to our records he has not returned to date.

The present certificate has been granted for legal rights.

Paris, December 27, 1945

Now all the more, she immersed herself in the development and the success, of the organization. She even considered dropping her plan to go to America.

Journey Four

Siecq to Ile de Ré

Chapter Fourteen

The people of Siecq were quick to resume the pre war activities. On May seventh, we heard that the Germans had capitulated, however the armistice was not going to be official until the next day, the eighth. The entire country began the long awaited celebration that came to be known as VE (Victory in Europe) day.

Time passed so slowly. The war was over and the other two children had left Siecq to return to their families on the island. I didn't want to be ungrateful, but still, I thought that I also should have been back with my family. I received an occasional letter from Paris. Mamie and Pepére had started writing also. The impression I had, was that my grandparents and my mother felt it would be better if I stayed in Siecq a little longer. Food was still scarce on the island, and the situation was not back to normal.

I asked Amie about my family's decision; she felt that they were right and that I could stay in Siecq as long as needed. In fact she seemed to be pleased. She and I started doing more things together. We went into the fields to gather dandelions and watercress, for salads. We visited her uncle and his family in a nearby village. We studied together, she her architecture, and me my catechism. I found out there was a lot more to learn than the mass in Latin. I had learned that by heart the year before, not just the responses, but the priest's part as well. I studied hard since my catechism class and I were due to celebrate our Solemn Communion soon.

Summer vacation passed and school began again. Christmas 1945 was much better than the previous ones. We exchanged gifts this time. I didn't have any money, so I had to make the gifts. For Monsieur Mechain I made a wooden whistle. Since I had learned to knit, when I was in the hospital, I decided to knit a pair of mittens for Amie's present. It was quite an undertaking since I had only knitted blanket squares. I did fine until I had to set up for the thumb. There I was lost. I went to the post office to enlist help from Jacques' mother. Unfortunately help was not all that I got. Jacques and another boy from school were there. In their way of thinking a nine-year-old boy was not supposed to knit. They teased me unmercifully, there and later at school; I managed to finish the mittens.

I presented them proudly to Amie just before we left for midnight mass. She said she was very pleased "even though one thumb was longer than the other". I had done my best; so I thought. The lesson of the day was that my best was not perfect. She went on to say, "regardless of the task in the future, I could not consider it completed until there was no chance of improving upon it". I was crushed! Our walk to church was under a cloud that stayed with me for weeks. That simple experience however, did teach me that my standards would have to be higher, if I was to please others.

I wondered if I should follow Amie's example. Even I could tell that she was not leading her life for herself. She derived pleasure from working to please others. I wasn't sure that I wanted to work toward that direction in life. We arrived at the church in silence.

January passed slowly. Midway through the month

of February 1946, Amie sat down to read a letter from my mother. She had barely finished the first paragraph when she began to weep. She held her hands out to me saying gently, "*Viens ici*". She then read the rest aloud. I was to go back to La Flotte. I would stay with Pepere and Mamie until maman came for me.

The next few days flew by; my meager possessions should not have taken more than two hours to pack. We took over two weeks just washing clothes and having shoes made. Amie and I visited her family and friends. Monsieur Mechain, though distant since our trip to Angoulême to deliver Papillon, was now spending more time around the dinner table. We made the rounds of his farms to say goodbye to those families.

Amie said she was worried about me taking the train to La Rochelle by myself, so she made plans to accompany me. She changed them at the last minute, not wanting to leave her father by himself. He was no longer in good health. I reassured her that I would be all right. After all I had traveled from Paris to La Rochelle when I was six. Now I was nine years old and this time I didn't have to fear the Gestapo, so there really was nothing to worry about.

I said goodbye to my schoolmates and to my friend Jacques. My romance with Therése had not blossomed into the love of the decade; still I went to her house for my farewell. We spent an hour or so in the garden house. This time we held hands while we talked, then we kissed goodbye, chaste kisses on the cheeks.

The next morning Amie and I walked to the station hand in hand. I carried only my book satchel and my few clothes wrapped in an old tablecloth, the four corners folded and tied in the middle, like a hobo's pack. Amie hugged me for a few moments. I gave her the customary three kisses on the cheeks, and boarded the train from Angoulême. It had stopped for a brief five minutes; just long enough to pick me up. I was the only passenger leaving Siecq. Amie and I waved until I left the window and sat down.

My compartment had only two other people in it. One was an elderly man the other was a nun. I was surprised to see the sister by herself. Generally, at least two sisters traveled together. Maybe the war had changed even that. The next stop was to be St. Jean D'Angely two hours away.

I peered over the edge of the windows watching the countryside pass rapidly by. I became excited with anticipation. A new chapter in my life was starting. It was as if the door to Ali Baba's cave had just opened. Instead of seeing treasures of gold and jewels, I saw wondrous happenings. My father and I would be reunited. He had been released from the concentration camp and was racing toward the island. He and I would reach La Palice just in time to take the ferry, and to arrive at Pepere's house together. I came out of my reverie thinking how real that had been. I knew that I had been wishing so hard; still I had so many things to tell him.

I knew that I should not let myself become emotional but thinking about the passing of the previous few years without him was really hard. That chapter had so much significance toward the development of the rest of my life. The Mechain family, seemingly with little personal reward, had allowed me to live, not to just exist. So many families in those times fought for the bare essentials, simply to ward off starvation. They gave me a fairly normal life without real fear of persecution. I was so aware that many children, especialy in the cities, some of my age some even younger, had reached that page of their lives on which was printed "*FIN*".

The Mechain family had taken me in when it was

dangerous for them to do so. I realized that I had not always been prudent or even smart. My episode with the gypsy could have cost Monsieur Mechain his farm, even his life. I did not know how much they were paid for my board if anything, somehow I didn't think that they would have taken it. Amie, though a bit strange and somewhat distant, was ready to help me with anything that I might need. Perhaps her distance was in preparation for this day of good-byes. She knew that I was there only for the duration of the war.

The "Good Sister" brought me out of my reveries by starting to quiz me. She wanted to know everything I had learned from my catechism. She asked if I had made my Solemn Communion? I told her not yet, I would have in a month or so but I was going home, so I would do that in La Flotte. The questions continued; at first I thought she was just bored and that she was testing me. Then I became somewhat suspicious. She really was not asking the questions like she knew the answers. Certainly a sister should have known the difference between *"ascension"* and *"assomption"*. I decided that she really was not a nun, but was disguised as one for her own purpose. That might have explained why she was traveling alone. When we arrived at La Rochelle she descended from the train and hurried off. I never saw her again.

This time Pepére met me at the train. I saw him on the quay, leaning on his cane, his beret jauntily perched to the right side of his head. I jumped onto the platform without help and ran to him. He had not seen me until I greeted him. He looked down through his ever-dirty glasses. One of the lenses had cracked since I had seen him last.

"We must hurry to catch the boat" was his greeting. I felt rebuffed, but I was too excited to let it bother me. We took a bus to La Palice. Almost three years had past since I had been there. The devastation from bombs was depressing. There was more rubble than buildings left standing. The passage to Sablanceau was quick but dangerous; the burned out skeletons of sunken ships bordered the channel on one side, and there were rumors of submerged mines on the other. The Micheline was running again and we made good time to La Flotte.

The reception I received from Mamie made up for the one I had from Pepére. The neighbors came to see me. I was not strong yet but I was so much better than the last time I had been in La Flotte. They all seemed glad to see me.

Soon I was registered in public school in La Flotte. Times were improving. I served mass in the centuries old church of *Sainte Catherine*. Instead of one altar boy, there were four. My new friend Jacques Romigereau was my age, he was very devout for a nine-year-old. He had committed to God that he would attend the seminary to become a priest.

Two other boys around twelve or thirteen, were also responsible for ringing the bells, announcing mass. The first Sunday, after mass, they convinced Jacques and me to go up the steeple to do something with the bell rope. We climbed the stairs to a platform, then a ladder to a smaller platform around the bells. We were used to ladders on the farms, so it wasn't that big of a challenge. However, when we reached the top, they pulled the ladder down and left, laughing. We yelled, to no avail. It was amazing how quickly people left the church grounds after mass. We sat for a while, trying to decide who would slide down the rope to get the ladder.

It sure seemed a lot further going down than it had going up. We got up again to look out of the openings. It was amazing how far we could see. We began counting the orange tiled roofs to pass the time. We thought, surely they would return to put the ladder back up. We must have debated for an hour with no decision as to who would go down the rope.

We knew we were late for lunch, and knew that our folks would be mad. I thought, here is another friend and his name is Jacques also, and already I was in trouble. Luckily, Jacques had an older brother whose parents sent him to look for him. He had been an altar boy a few years before and was familiar with this rite of passage, which all new altar boys had to endure. That prank had been going on for decades. He went right to the belfry and called for Jacques. We yelled down at him to rescue us. He patted us both on the back and told us that, someday soon we would have a chance to do that to someone else.

I told Pepére of my misadventure; he laughed telling me that the same thing happened to him as a boy, when he was still going to church. After lunch on Sunday afternoons we went to see Charlie Chaplin movies in an old converted barn.

Twice a day on my way to and from school I passed by the Café Poncé or it might have been the Café du Port, owned by Monsieur Poncé. Each afternoon a big red chow dog chased me. I tried to compare that to my encounter with the gander in Siecq and of my philosophy concerning the dragon. Reality was, that fear of that dog was overpowering, so I ran. One day he caught me and bit me, literally removing a chunk of flesh from my thigh. That time I did cry. Someone in the Café saw the commotion and brought me inside, sat me on a barstool and gave me a glass of beer to drink while I was being bandaged with a white napkin. The beer had to have been the vilest tasting potion on earth.

I was taken to the sister's school to be bandaged again. It was the same school that I had attended a few years before. Since there was still not a doctor in the town, the sisters were considered to be nurses, many had medical first aid training.

From then on I went three blocks out of the way to get to school. I passed in front of the church instead of the café.

Ile de Ré was said to be the working man's *Riviera;* many homes were summer homes, belonging to Parisians. My second cousin Guy Paul, his mother and sister began coming again for summer vacation. His father Lucien was my godfather who was away fighting in Indo-China. They also, came from Paris to stay with his grandmother Alexandrine, Pepére's sister, and her husband Alexandre. Tonton, as I called his grandfather, was a World War I amputee. He had lost his right leg at mid thigh from gangrene after a shrapnel wound.

He was a bitter man, short of patience and short of temper. Whether it was due to his infirmity or if he would have been like that anyway we did not know. He supplemented his pension by caning chairs. I watched him in fascination. I even asked him to teach me the art sometime, but he didn't have the patience. He would let us watch for a few minutes then generally would tell us to "go play on your two good legs".

Guy Paul and I were the same age and we were both in love with his neighbor across the street, the cute blond from Paris, Denise, she was also our age.

Pepere and I passed the time by working in the gardens. Every other day we walked to the *boulangerie* to buy fresh bread. But before stopping on the way back, we walked to the end of the breakwater that protected the entrance to the harbor. I enjoyed sitting at the base of the white lighthouse, watching boats come in and out of the narrow opening. On the way back I hurried ahead to look in the barred window of the one room jail, to see if it held anyone new.

Daily I gathered snails for Mamie's flour barrel. She kept a small wooden barrel approximately thirty inches high and eighteen inches across a third full of flour. Garden snails had to be placed in there for several weeks to cleanse themselves before being cooked for a gourmet Sunday meal. During exceptionally low tides we went to Pepére's oyster park where we gathered oysters, *petoncle* (scallops) and large eels called *concros*. Much of our food still had to come from nature.

The following week we worked at trying to retrieve copper bottomed pots and pans and a huge copper cauldron that he had dropped down a seldom used well in the garden. He had decided that under no condition, would he allow the Germans to melt them down to make shell casings to be used against our allies. We did get the pots but I was unable to bring up the cauldron.

Vacation flew by; Guy Paul, Denise and I spent many days at the beach. I made my solemn communion on June 20th in the church of *Sainte Catherine*, the church of my baptism. Guy Paul and Denise went back to Paris and I started school again.

Journey Five

Ile de Ré to Paris
to New York

Chapter Fifteen

Serge and maman had stayed in Paris. He in school, she still even more involved with the "Union of Jewish Students". During the summer, she had attended a world conference in the Alpine village of Uriage. The highlight of the conference to many, was the visit of David Ben-Gurion. She was certain that he was to become a person history would remember. Indeed, he became the first Prime Minister of the State of Israel.

The mountain air was charged with energy and hope. The brotherhood and the focus of all these young people made a lasting impression on her. Even as a Gentile, she was accepted beyond her greatest hope as one of the leaders of this wonderful organization.

She had worked for many months with the group, when she decided that she should also think of her family. It had been over a year since she had seen me. Many of the American soldiers billeted in the mansion next door had left several months before, to either go home or to fight the Japanese.

Earlier in the year she had gone to the American embassy to obtain a passport. She had been married twice, once to a French national, and then to a Hungarian naturalized French following her marriage to the American. There was some question as to the status of her citizenship.

Weeks of research, then deliberation by the authorities dragged on. The twentieth of March 1946 arrived; she was given a document by the Minister of Justice addressed to the Consul General of the United States, stating that she had not regained her French citizenship. Therefore, she was still an American citizen and had been, throughout the war. Obtaining the passport would take time.

Maman was thrilled; she wrote Pepére to put me on the train in September right after my birthday. He was to take me to La Rochelle and she would meet me at the station in Paris. She had planned to come to La Flotte to get me, but she could not take the time. She told them that I was now accustomed to traveling alone, so it would be all right.

Maman went to see her friends in Paris, to tell them of her plans. They greeted her with mixed responses and with a flurry of advice and caution. She acknowledged that she had many friends in France, even some in high positions. Her life could probably be good, if she was patient. On the other hand, in the United States she knew only three people; the Moores in California and Ed Law in Connecticut. Ed had been a student from Yale, studying political science when she was a student at the Sorbonne. Still, if she could give us security, good nourishment and comfort, she would have succeeded in honoring her promise to my father.

Her decision made, she had a lot to accomplish in a short time. She went back to the American embassy to inquire about the progress of a passport and visa for the three of us. She had been to purchase our ocean liner tickets, two months in advance. She was turned away, unable to buy them without a visa.

She had also been told that she could not take Francs out of the country, so she bought a few diamonds to add to the jewelry that she had managed to hide from the Germans. Nellie, a student whom she had helped, told her that her father was a jeweler who could make her a ring since she could not carry loose diamonds. They would have been considered contraband and therefore confiscated. Maman agreed to a ring, a brooch and ear-rings. Later, she found out that her good friend had taken a very fine diamond to be used for the center, and replaced it with an inferior one. Maman was so hurt and disillusioned by the greed of one she thought to be a friend.

Maman received a telephone call from the American embassy in mid August, saying that we would be unable to go at this time. It seemed that there was a quota. Even though she was a citizen, she had not returned in twenty years, therefore she would have to be treated like an immigrant. The following week she heard that Serge's papers were not complete. He would be unable to receive a passport until all was in order. She had feared that something like that would happen with Serge. The Germans had confiscated his identity papers, and had not returned all the documents she had shown them.

Immediately, she wrote Doctor Moore describing our predicament. He had been working with the State Department in the United States. He had to furnish a letter of responsibility, acknowledging that he was financially capable of supporting us if maman was unable to work. Upon receiving her letter, he went to his friend Senator Wayne Morse, who quickly introduced a bill in the United States Senate waving the quota requirement for our entry. After that every document was expedited and maman was called to pick up our passport and visa.

That taken care of, she was made aware of a new problem. She had to leave France within ten days or her visa would be void. Even more important she would forfeit her American citizenship, and mine as well.

She had to decide what to do with Serge. He was now sixteen and his American citizenship had been invalidated. That appeared to be an insurmountable problem for the short amount of time that we had. He would be unable to come with us. She decided that once she was in the United States, with the help available she would be able to get Serge to join us. But if she lost her citizenship, it may take years to regain it, if ever.

Serge would stay with Pepére and Mamie until his safe passage was guaranteed. We, on the other hand, continued working on another of my journeys.

My trip to Paris had been uneventful. Pepere went with me to the railroad station in La Rochelle, placed me in the care of the conductor for a small *pourboire*. It was probably nowhere near as much as had been in the envelope given me by Doctor Eva. Maman met me at the station. We descended to the metro and we went to our old apartment.

I walked around our apartment, memories of my father coming back at every turn. Maman and I had a long serious conversation the next day. She told me that she felt he would never return. We did not have any proof that he was dead, but it had been too long, he would have been released and found us by now. So, we must now plan our lives without him. I should always keep good memories of him, as he had been a good and sensitive man. I should always remain proud of him since he had been talented and intent on helping other people gain their freedom. In fact doing so cost him his own freedom and ultimately his life. I wouldn't go in his study, it hurt too much.

Our steamer trunk was shipped to Le Havre two days in advance. Maman was finishing her packing. Mine was finished; I had a new valise and my leather school bag.

Serge and one of his friends helped us with our luggage to the Gare Saint Lazare. There, we boarded the train for Le Havre. The last thing I remember of that train trip was, standing in line for the restaurant car throughout the first sitting, then being told that we did not have the right tickets to eat. We went without food again. I took an oath, this would be the last time for me and for my family, whenever I had one. I would make sure that no one dear to me would ever be hungry again.

We arrived in Le Havre. Pepére and Mamie were waiting to meet us. They had come from La Rochelle to see us off. We only had a short time to be together, since we had to board before dark. We all went from the train station to the harbor. We sat in a restaurant looking out toward the harbor; several freighters were tied up within our range of vision, flags of various countries flying. Then I saw a huge gray American ship. The name SS Washington was painted on the bow.

Maman told us how wonderful the passage would be. She had used almost all of our remaining cash for first class tickets. We said our good-byes, maman and I carrying our bags quickly through customs, and then up the long gangplank. Pepére and Mamie left us going to Paris to sell our furniture, vacate the apartment, and take Serge with them to La Flotte.

The date was October 6, 1946. We looked for our cabin. We realized then, that the travel agent might have made a little money on this first class transaction. There was no first class! The SS Washington had been reconfigured as a troop ship during the war. Large dormitories with multilevel bunks had replaced the luxurious cabins. That also explained why the ship was now battleship gray instead of as the pictures showed it with a beautiful black hull and white and red trim.

Women were assigned to one side of the ship on each deck and the men on the other. I was to be two decks below my mother with a group of men. Maman, upset, went to see the officer in charge of assigning sleeping accommodations. There was no problem, he simply moved me to the same deck as my mother and moved another man to my old bunk.

We had not even left the dock, and we were going to eat. Given the choice, maman selected the first sitting for our meals. She also, didn't want the food to run out as it had on the train. We should not have worried. I soon found out there was enough! The tables were dressed with stacks of bread, butter, salads and fruit. The entrees were huge; I could not believe the amount of food taken back to the kitchen to be thrown to the fish. For months maman had suffered from malnutrition. She had even been close to starvation; many in other countries and even some in France had died of hunger. I knew people that could still use this food. I was appalled.

The menu was written only in English; I certainly could not read it. Now I wasn't sure that going to America was going to be as great as maman had told me. I let her know my thoughts. She responded by scolding me saying that I was already in a New World, I would have to become accustomed to the language and the new ways. I should not criticize what I didn't understand.

We took the elevator to the promenade deck, found a place by the rail like the rest of the passengers, and watched. At eight o'clock, four tugs attached themselves, pulled and pushed us out of the harbor. Soon, we were under way. Even with all the excitement, we were both exhausted. We went to our respective bunks.

A tall man in the bunk next to me spoke to me in English; of course I had to say "*Je ne comprend pas*". That would be the first time of many on this voyage. I didn't like that, by nature I was inquisitive and wanted to know what was being said. I was going to have to learn English in a hurry. He smiled but he didn't pursue the conversation. I lay awake for a short time saying my prayers, wishing Mamie, Pepére and Serge a good and safe trip back to Ré, I prayed also that Serge would be able to join us in America soon.

I awoke; I searched for any type of rocking, something similar to ferry boat crossings. There was no movement. Even though the ship was large, we should have felt some sense of motion. I got up, dressed, and went to find maman. She was outside my compartment door talking excitedly to my neighbor of the night before. She told me we had been in Southampton since midnight and we were taking on another five hundred passengers. In a few hours we would be underway for Cork in Ireland, then on to the United States and our new home.

We had breakfast, then went on deck to look at England. I saw a ship even bigger than ours. Maman said that it was the "Queen Elizabeth". We saw a lot of activity in the harbor but no sign of sunken ships or evidence of bombings. Noon came and finally we were under way just in time for lunch. We had our assigned places but now my bunk neighbor was sitting next to maman. She said that he was from someplace called Texas.

Again I was overwhelmed by the enormous servings. I ate only little bits. We thought that we had enough food in Siecq. Compared to many other areas we did, but it was nothing to what we saw on this table. It was all good, but my stomach had shrunk inside.

The ship began rocking during lunch. Some of the passengers were forced to leave the table. We finished our meal and went back up to the promenade deck. Our new friend bought me a beverage in a strange looking bottle with a straw. He called it "Coca-Cola". I had never used a straw, but I caught on very quickly. It had a terrible flavor. I managed to drink a part of it then, accidentally, as I leaned over the rail it slipped through my fingers into the sea far below.

We went to our respective compartments to clean up and dress for dinner. The only suit I had was the gray suit with short pants that I had worn that summer for my solemn communion. I would take it off at night and lay it flat under my mattress to keep the creases in as Pepére had taught me.

The seas started building because of a winter storm. Many people were seasick. I was accustomed to the ferry crossing that sometimes became pretty rough. Maman became ill, the ship's doctor said it was fatigue and the concern of leaving Serge behind. He ordered her to bed for three days. I was somewhat lost. I watched people playing shuffleboard on deck and cards in the salon. The man from Texas lost interest in me pretty quickly. Probably since I did not speak English or even more likely since my mother was sick. The next time I saw him he had moved from our table and was sitting next to another woman.

An English lady assigned to our table spoke fluent French; she supervised my welfare for the next three days. She introduced me to tea and *petit beurre* biscuits every afternoon. It was a pleasant custom. When the doctor told maman she could get up the three of us continued the ritual. On the fourth day of the storm I became seasick. My pride suffered a certain amount of damage. I believed that I surrendered to *mal de mer* solely because of all the sick people around, it just could not have been the motion of the ship. I was fortunate, my discomfort only lasted until I lost my breakfast, after that I seemed to be fine.

Two days before arriving in New York maman sent messages to her friends in the States. We speculated as to who would meet us, if anyone. Surely Doctor Moore would not come all the way from California. Maybe Ed could come, we had looked in an Atlas before we left; Connecticut did not appear to be very far from New York.

Our excitement mounted as we approached the harbor on the evening of the thirteenth. Customs would not allow us to enter until the next day, so the ship anchored for the night. A strike of the luggage handlers did nothing to expedite our disembarking. We walked around the deck a few times, then I went below to pack my things so that I would be ready to disembark in the morning.

Customs agents and a few policemen boarded the ship early in the morning. We made three lines, French in one dining room; English in another and Americans were to just file out to the promenade deck after having their passports stamped. Maman accustomed to queues had told me to get up early and bring my luggage. Our turn came quickly; we were both on the same passport due to my status as a minor. The customs agent looked at the pictures and then looked at us, then he said something to maman; the picture of me had been taken when I was younger. She started in English then switched to French. I could tell she was angry, but more than that, she was scared.

Another customs agent came and escorted us to a small room. I became scared. What was happening? Things like this should not happen. The people ahead of us had walked right through. I asked maman what was happening? She told me to be quiet. The agent seeing that she was excited, spoke in French this time. He showed her the date on the passport, telling her that it had expired the previous day and that we would have to return to France.

She told him that was impossible. We had sold everything there, to buy tickets for this voyage, and we had no money left. She had survived bombings, evaded arrests and used her wits to travel when travel was forbidden. She was not going to allow the date on a passport to alter her plans for our future. Fear made her think more clearly. She said, "Anyway, we were on the ship in time and if it had gone into the harbor yesterday as it should have, we would have made it ashore before it expired." "Then another thing" she went on, " was this not an American ship? Was it not anchored in the mouth of a river, inside territorial waters? So were we not really in the United States?"

The expiration date was October 13, 1946, four years to the day that the Gestapo had arrested my father.

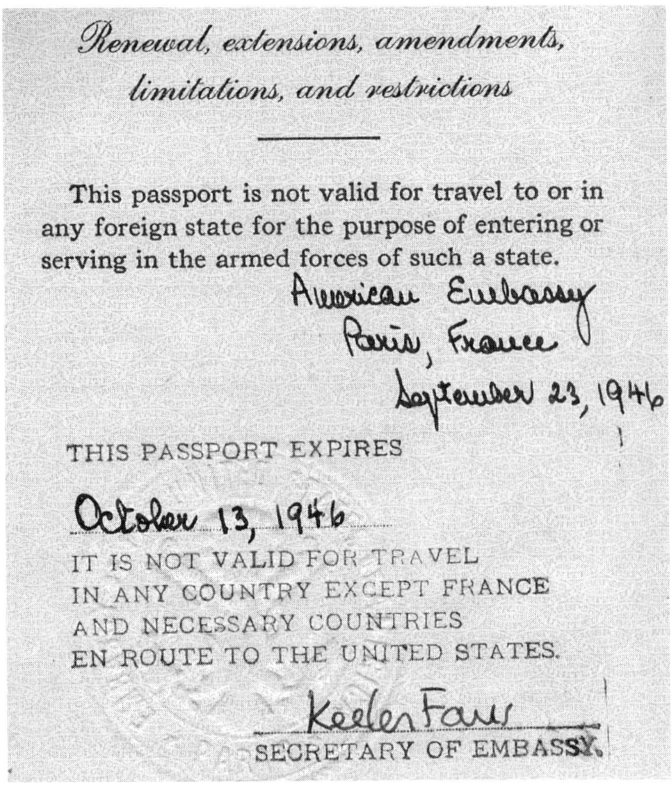

Renewal, extensions, amendments, limitations, and restrictions

This passport is not valid for travel to or in any foreign state for the purpose of entering or serving in the armed forces of such a state.

American Embassy
Paris, France
September 23, 1946

THIS PASSPORT EXPIRES

October 13, 1946

IT IS NOT VALID FOR TRAVEL
IN ANY COUNTRY EXCEPT FRANCE
AND NECESSARY COUNTRIES
EN ROUTE TO THE UNITED STATES.

Keeler Faus
SECRETARY OF EMBASSY.

Reproduction of original document

Evidently maman was very convincing. We watched the expressions of the customs agent. He seemed a little taken aback after listening to mother's declaration. He did not say a word for several moments, finally he smiled and told her she was right, but had we not been citizens of the United States of America we would have been sent back. It was nice to have been French, but already I saw the advantages to being an American and I was proud. Still I was concerned that our entire future rested solely on the whim of one man. That seemed like too much power for one person!

The SS Washington was escorted through the fog by a school of small tugs. We were still on the promenade deck trying to get a look at the famous *Statue de la Liberty*. The fog was too dense. I would not see it until many years later.

We had to leave the promenade to go to the disembarkation deck where the gangplank was to be connected. A sea of people milled about on the dock waiting for their families. Emotions flowed, greetings and cheers were shouted from the ship as on the dock. Our joy was mixed with the sadness that Serge was not able to be with us on such an important and unforgettable day. Maman searched the crowd and saw no one she knew until she happened to look up. Straddling a brace into the steel girders was Ed, a policeman yelling at him to get down from his perch. Maman saw him and then yelled "There is Ed, there is Ed!" He spotted us and started coming down. When he joined his father who had driven with him, maman saw Mary Mitchell Moore standing together with them. She had come all the way from California to welcome us.

I had no idea exactly how far California was but I had seen it on the globe. It was almost as far across land as we had been on the sea. How wonderful it was to come this far and to have someone meet us. We had wondered what we would do once we arrived, if no one had been there. Our idea was to go to a hotel and from there we would make our plans. We finished with customs that searched our bags again, then went to the car. I sat in the front seat with Uncle Abe, as I was to call Ed's father. We all fit easily in the large four-door Packard.

Uncle Abe drove for some time and stopped at a restaurant. Ed put a coin in the stand on the sidewalk while explaining the function of a parking meter. I asked where the money went after the pipe that it was on filled up. He said it went to a bigger pipe that ran under the street, then it went straight to city hall. We sat in a restaurant booth, Ed put money in a small machine on the wall, and then music came from another machine on the floor called a jukebox. I asked where those coins went? He told me very seriously that the pipes in the wall took all the money to the bank on the corner. We had only been in the United States two hours and already I was learning new and astonishing things; and I believed them!

Our meal finished we drove Aunt Mitch, as Mrs. Moore wanted me to call her, to Grand Central Station. She would take the train back to California with several stops to visit friends along the way.

We drove through New York streets, looking into store windows at clothing and toys, and on sidewalk displays of fresh fruit and vegetables in quantities that I had never imagined. We drove onto a beautiful highway divided by wide expanses of grass and trees, almost all the way to Shelton, Connecticut. Uncle Abe was very proud of this road he called the Merrit Parkway. We exited close to New Haven just at dusk. Lights from dozens of automobiles were blinding, what a difference this was from the hooded car lights in France. The most fascinating sight was that of homes with every room illuminated, they looked so warm and inviting. Even after the war we had only been allowed lights in two rooms at the same time.

Within a half-hour we drove on the bridge crossing the Housatonic River that brought us to the middle of Shelton. Uncle Abe drove up a steep winding street to the top of a hill and stopped at a big beautiful house overlooking the town. Every room, including an upstairs verandah, was also brightly lit.

Aunt Mae, their other son Raymond and his wife Ruth ran to the car to welcome us. Ed made a sweeping gesture encompassing the house saying "this is our home and it is now yours for as long as you want to stay, I hope you like it". What was there not to like? The house and the view looked like they came from the pages of a magazine. Serge would have been so happy here. I would write to him with a complete description.

Supper was ready; we sat in a beautiful dining room with two crystal chandeliers. Then went to the living room for cakes and real coffee, just like on the ship. We sat around the fireplace while Ed played the piano and sang about "Poor little lambs that had lost their way, Bah, Bah, Baaaah". They talked way into the night, Aunt Mae told me to follow her upstairs. I slept on a nice bed instead of a bunk on the ship.

The next morning Uncle Abe wanted to know if I would eat some grapefruit. I had seen some on the ship, but had never tasted one before. Uncle Abe set a stool next to the cutting table for me to watch. First, he cut it in half and separated the segments. He took a tool and cored it, than poured two teaspoons of honey in the hole, then topped it with a candied cherry. The procedure was to take a little honey with each section. I still prepare it that way.

Journey Six

New York to Connecticut
to New Hampshire to California

Chapter Sixteen

The next few days flew. Ed had played football at Yale so he bought me a strange looking ball that was not round. Ray on the other hand had played basketball at Harvard so he bought me a basketball. Those I had seen in Paris. They both took me to a football game in New Haven at the Yale bowl. I had absolutely no idea what all those men were doing on the field. It looked pretty senseless. They just kept running and knocking each other down. It was cold and I was bored but I was so happy to be there. I would learn about football someday.

After the game we went to a little restaurant just across from the Yale Bowl called the "Red Lobster". Their specialty was a "lobster roll". That meat was so sweet, with lots of butter. Whenever we went to New Haven we stopped and bought me a lobster roll.

Uncle Abe took me to his factory; it was really two factories in one. One made all kinds of baskets: picnic, laundry, purses and others. The other part of the factory made tools, mostly wood planes. I was turned over to Al the foreman, while Uncle Abe took care of business. Al found me some pieces of wood and nails. I drew a picture of an airplane hangar on a piece of wood. He cut me the pieces, gave me nails and a hammer and assigned me to a workbench. I stayed there until my hangar was assembled.

Al took us, the hangar and me to the spray booth where they varnished the baskets. The painter sprayed my hangar, placed it in an oven to let it dry, then took me and my hangar to the main office where Ray was working.

Soon Uncle Abe came for me and we went to a small diner that looked like a railroad car. He had me take my hangar in, telling everyone that I had just made it. I could not speak English but I was starting to understand the meaning of some words.

Uncle Abe decided that I should surprise my mother by saying something in English so he taught me a little song. It went like this:

Morning Glory bright and gay
Why so proudly fade away?
Won't you tell me if you may?
Why you quickly fade away?

It was not easy but I learned it all in one day. Mother was surprised and pleased.

The next day mother and I went to New Haven with Ed where his office was. He had a small business manufacturing some thing called a "Smoker's Robot". It was an ashtray with a built in cigarette holder, a small tube two feet long coming from the bottom of the holder to a mouthpiece. This gadget was intended to let you smoke in bed without fear of fire.

Ed put me to work individually boxing the Smoker's Robot. We were there three or four hours, he gave me some coins for my work probably less than one dollar. Nevertheless, this was the first money I had ever earned. I had worked in France but my reward was food and shelter. Now I would be able to buy anything I wanted with my money.

That night at supper, mother mentioned that she had found Wayne's address in New Hampshire. She asked no one in particular how far Lancaster was. Several at the table answered "not too far". Uncle Abe said to call him and tell him we are coming. After supper mother was shown the wonders of locating someone anywhere in the country by dialing "0" on the telephone. Mother and Wayne spoke and made plans to have us come visit. He seemed so happy to hear from mother that he said his sister, Alpha, would be glad to welcome us the next day.

The next morning we got up early; had a big breakfast. Uncle Abe, Ed, mother and I got in the Packard with a big picnic basket that Aunt Mae had prepared. She decided to stay at home since the lady who did the laundry was coming that day. We had been in Shelton ten days, now we were going on a trip. It didn't take us long to get into the country. The leaves on the trees were beautiful. I didn't realize that there were so many shades of brown, orange and yellow. Ed said that it was really getting too late to see the beauty that was normally available. Many trees had already lost their leaves.

Ed was a human road atlas. He knew what each town was going to be in advance. He said we were leaving Connecticut and going into the next state. He taught me to say Massachusetts before I learned many simpler words. I must have repeated it over a hundred times. Finally he said I had it right. There were so many small towns and the roads were winding. We stopped at a roadside stand selling apple cider. Within a few hours we left Massachusetts and our walking atlas said we were entering New Hampshire.

I was puzzled; we had crossed two borders and had not seen any gates. There were no guards to check our papers. We simply drove by a sign that said, "Welcome". What a wonderful way to travel. This really was freedom.

The countryside in New Hampshire was different from the other two. There seemed to be many more farms.

They were a beautiful sight, even if they almost all looked the same. The houses were white with green trim, nearby was always a big red barn and a tall white tower that Ed called a "silo".

The big car went up into the White Mountains effortlessly. The winding roads were like I had never seen before. We would pass big trucks going up the hills, and then they would blow their horns wanting us to let them pass going down the next hill.

Late in the afternoon, we crested a hill and immediately drove down into a sea of fog. Mother suggested that we stop in the next town of Whitefield to telephone Wayne for directions. He had said that his sister's farm was at least five miles from Lancaster but we didn't know in which direction.

We were to meet Wayne in the village, from there he would guide us to his sister's house. We drove into town keeping a sharp eye out for someone that no one other than mother knew. She spotted him standing in front of his old Plymouth. He was not in uniform any longer but mother said that she would have recognized his stature anywhere.

The introductions completed, mother and I went in Wayne's car to lead the way.

We arrived at the large farmhouse where I was introduced to John a year older than me, Priscilla my age and Peter two years younger. Their last name was Alden, which at the time had no meaning. But by the time that we returned to Shelton, Ed had told us the story of the Pilgrims, John Alden and Pricilla.

Our stay was pleasant; the children took me under their care and in spite of the language barrier we managed to have a good time. A farm here was not like a farm that I knew in France. They used machines to milk the cows that all looked the same. They were called Jerseys. They used tall concrete silos to store the feed for winter, while we had made huge haystacks. The three days we spent there went by very fast and I learned so much. .

Uncle Abe and I spent the first morning back going to a big market in New Haven to buy two cases of apples. Aunt Mae and Ruth had made a huge pot of a red sugary substance. We spent the rest of the day washing and dipping apples for that evening. Soon after dark the doorbell began to ring. Grotesquely masked and dressed children, carrying large sacks bewildered me. I was told that this day was called Halloween. All kids had to do, was dress up and go to every house and yell "trick or treat". Then prizes and gifts would come. What a great country this was! It went on late into the night and almost all the apples were gone.

Aunt Mae took me to a movie while mother went to New Haven to work on getting Serge into the country. This day was my introduction to cowboys and to the Wild West where we were supposed to go. I was really looking forward to that part of the country. Mother came back that night demoralized. It was going to take almost a year for Serge to be allowed a visa. Something had to be done. She would try again from California.

The first two weeks of December went fast. Uncle Abe took me to his factory for a few hours daily, usually from ten to two, that way we were able to have lunch in the diner on main street. The pretty waitress, who served us, always managed to place her hand on his shoulder and smile at him. He usually gave her paper money for tips while other customers gave her coins.

Mother translated the last letter from Uncle Russell; he wished that we could arrive there before Christmas. They were anxious for us to be there to get settled before Uncle Russell had to go back to Portland, Oregon to teach at his new University. They had to change their plans, since we had been in Shelton almost two months, while we had been expected to go with Aunt Mitch.

This wonderful family had accepted us as members. It would be difficult to leave them. We had just left our family in France. I told mother that I missed Serge and my grandparents. She told me that learning to deal with separations was only another step in becoming an adult. Acquaintances may turn into friendships, but they can only be called friendships when they last as hers had for twenty years with the Moores.

Our good-byes said, Uncle Abe drove us to the commuter train to New York. Ed would ride with us to Grand Central Station to make sure we boarded the correct train for Oakland, California. We didn't travel first class; we were in a "Pullman" sleeper car. It was really kind of fun and it looked like first class to me. How could it be better? The train was not like the ones I had been on in France. The seats were much more comfortable. The dining car had plenty of food and the utensils were made of silver.

Passengers were friendly, trying to start conversations with us. I was now able to understand the meaning of many English words. I could not carry on a conversation because I was still bashful about saying the words that I had learned. I knew that I must sound as silly to the Americans as they did to me trying to speak French. Soon, though, I would just go ahead and do it.

I tried to remember the names of many cities we passed through. There was Omaha, then Salt Lake City, Reno and Oakland. I had missed the ones in the East. But the farther west we went the more interest I had. I looked out of the window, hoping to see Indians and cowboys. Not one came riding up on a horse.

The passengers began to disembark in Oakland, running to meet family and friends. The conductor handed our luggage down to a "Red Cap", I thought that it was strange that we would name a man after his hat. He started walking quickly to the station following the crowd. Mother asked him to wait; someone should be meeting us. He didn't seem too happy but he waited a few moments. We looked for Uncle Russell or Aunt Mitch; neither was visible. The Red Cap started walking again.

Almost every one had now left the concourse we were on. It was impossible that they would not have met us here. After all, Aunt Mitch traveled all the way across the country to meet us in New York, surely Pacific Grove could not be too far. We knew they had a car and Aunt Mitch did the driving from Oregon to California at least twice a year. There must have been an accident.

This was our first time completely on our own in these big United States. We did not feel fear, but had a large amount of apprehension. The Red Cap told us to take the ferry to San Francisco then a taxi to the train station to board a train to Pacific Grove.

The ferry was much bigger and the ride was a little longer than the one from La Palice to Sablanceaux. I was so happy to be back on the water. One of the passengers showed me the big rock of Alcatraz and explained that some of the worst men in the country were imprisoned there. The salt air filled my lungs just as the air seven thousand miles away on *Ile de Ré* had. If I had not been so exited about a new home I would have been homesick.

We made it to the train station still hoping to find Uncle Russell or Aunt Mitch if not both. Our disappointment grew, as no one came. Mother had had a relapse of her illness and was burning with fever. She forced herself to purchase our tickets. Immediately after she found a bench and told me that she had to lie down. I tried to find a doctor; I went to a Travelers Aid kiosk but was not able to make myself understood enough for the lady to call a doctor. There is so much difference between the French word *docteur* and the English doctor. Well no matter, I would not leave her alone. Even in this wonderful country, I was still afraid that someone would take our luggage as she slept. I worried about her, I tried to wake her, and she would rouse for a few seconds then immediately go back to sleep.

I had a few quarters in my pocket so I bought food and drink at the counter in the station. I woke her long enough to drink some juice, then she lay back down. Time for the train came closer; I shook her hard enough to wake her. She managed to walk to our train and collapsed in her seat. A kind man helped me get a Red Cap to bring the luggage aboard. I gave him my last two quarters.

The conductor yelled something that sounded like "Boooad", then the train lurched a few times taking the slack out of the couplings. We gained momentum quickly until we reached our running speed,then the lights dimmed. I sat back in my seat watching mother sleep. She had worked so hard and endured so much to make sure that we would be here to begin the last of our journeys to freedom.

I stared out of the window wondering how I had managed to end up on this train, going to a new home, without my father that I missed so, and without my brother. I thought again of the thousands of children who had been separated from their parents then taken to camps never to return. They had been innocent too, maybe even more so than me. Why had so many people helped me? Why was I here? Why had I been spared?

My reveries were interrupted by the lights of small multicolored Christmas trees shining brightly, in almost every house along the tracks, as the train slowed through the outskirts of towns.

Mother roused finally; almost as the conductor came to the car calling out that Pacific Grove would be the next stop. I started pulling down our luggage from the overhead racks. The station was illuminated well enough for us to see Aunt Mitch whom I recognized from New York, and a man with her, dressed in knickers and wearing a beret. He hugged and kissed us both going from one to the other time after time while Aunt Mitch stood in the background. He was a jolly looking man, like pictures I had seen of Santa Claus, rosy cheeks, bushy white eyebrows, but no beard.

He helped get our luggage from the train and loaded the car. Aunt Mitch took her turn to greet us with much less enthusiasm. She drove, she said she always drove. She told us that they had not met us in San Francisco because it was much better for us to learn to be self-reliant. We were in the United States now, Americans, and we should take care of ourselves like other Americans.

We were a bit puzzled, we both thought we had done pretty well going over seven thousand miles by ourselves on top of surviving for four years in an occupied country. We had to be grateful, so we smiled. Uncle Russell on the other hand said that she had had a terrible time keeping him from going to meet us.

We arrived at "La Petite Maison", in just a few minutes. Uncle Russell and I unloaded our bags and took them to our room in front of the house. A log crackled as it burned in the large living room fireplace. Next to the dining room door stood a Christmas tree decorated with colored balls and other hanging ornaments but no lights. The base of the tree was covered with colorfully wrapped gifts.

Aunt Mitch had gone right to the kitchen and made cocoa for us to have with a slice of plum pudding she had made earlier. The dishes washed, she said it was time for bed. That night we slept in the same bed. Though I was tired I could not go right to sleep. I asked mother why Aunt Mitch was mad at us. She answered me with the thought that it was not anger but maybe disappointment that we had not come with her two months before.

The next morning was December 24th, 1946. Aunt Mitch took me to the store to buy American clothes. It seemed to be important to her that I didn't look different from other boys my age. She bought me blue jeans and a red checkered western shirt. The afternoon we spent walking around the wild garden looking at the plants. Aunt Mitch came out to get me to help her make up a new bed. My room was going to be the dining room that was generally not used.

This was the first Christmas that I didn't go to midnight mass. Instead, Doctor Fisher and his wife Anne, came for a party. We opened a few of the gifts; the rest would wait until Christmas morning.

Morning came and I headed for the gifts. I was told that in this house we would act very civilized, breakfast came first and after the dishes were washed and put away, we could go to the living room to open gifts. I hurried through my first flapjacks smeared with butter and honey, a real western breakfast I was told. I learned where the dishes went since that would be part of my duties.

We eventually opened the rest of the presents. I wanted to tear into the packages but the mood had been set so I carefully opened the present that I had been handed. Of course this would not really be any different from the way that I had previously been brought up. Patience, reserve and formality were to be my direction. Two more shirts, another pair of jeans and a gingerbread man made up my gift list. I was really pleased until I was told to share the gingerbread man with everyone. Trying to please I carefully divided it so everyone could have an almost equal amount. That I could do. I had been so concerned with the equal division of food for four years that it was almost second nature to visualize something and divide it by the number of people in the room.

We did have a very good meal. Dessert was a home made, authentic apple-strudel. Aunt Mitch spent several hours making it giving me the history of the German dessert. At dinner she told me she had made it in my honor. It was to be my first step in forgiving the Germans for what had happened. I was "an American and all that *stuff* was in the past". I looked at mother who turned completely white; she started to say something but instead threw her napkin on the table, got up and left the room.

Uncle Russell rose to go after her but was told to sit down with a following quip, "it was a shame that a woman of breeding had such poor manners".

The next day mother stayed in her room and read. She was so upset. I was worried about her again. In France she may have been scared or exasperated but that was because of enemies, here she was among friends and she felt she had been insulted. She could not understand what she had done to Aunt Mitch to incur her wrath.

Uncle Russell spoke with her at length trying to make her feel better. I don't know how that went.

Between Christmas and New Year's eve Aunt Mitch took me to the store to buy school supplies and two more shirts. New Year's day turned out to be just another day.

Chapter Seventeen

The next Monday, January 6, 1947 was my first day of school in America.

Aunt Mitch and my mother escorted me to school. I was enthralled by the big concrete and brick building. This was a far cry from the village schools I had attended in France. Even the school in Paris had not been this large. I knew immediately that I would like it.

We spent over an hour in the principal's office. The papers with my name already on them indicated that we had been expected. Toward the end of our interview the principal sent for Miss Keith, a fifth grade teacher. My English was improving but still not good enough to test so he asked her to give me mimeographed arithmetic tests. I was able to get every problem right. So she gave me sixth grade work, I got that right too. They felt that I could do seventh grade math but since I was just ten they decide to place me in the fifth grade just to finish out the year. It had something to do with the "social growth of my young life," or something like that.

Miss Keith introduced me to the children in her class. It seemed that I would be accepted, at least for the first week. I learned the pledge to the flag well enough to lead it on Friday morning. Another Philip, with a different spelling from the one in France proudly told me that his mother also was French. She had come as a child over twenty years before.

Miss Keith's mother was also French. Maybe for that reason, she seemed able to understand the subtle differences in me from the American kids. A daily morning snack consisted of a carton of milk and two "Graham" crackers. I was given the responsibility of passing out the "Graham" crackers. That created a problem with Kenneth who had been the "Graham cracker monitor". During recess he came to me and told me that "tonight after school" he and I would meet.

I took him literally and met him on the playground after school. He met me with a punch to the head. I had never fought before and knew nothing about it. In fact I could not ever remember seeing a fight in any school in France. My impulse was to get back up and wrestle. We wrestle as a test of strength and quickness but always in fun. I got up just in time to parry a punch with my head and decided I didn't like that. By then a crowd of fifth and sixth graders had gathered and formed a circle. There were calls of "get the Frenchy", followed by a lot of laughter.

The teacher on yard duty came, took us both by the arm and marched us to the principal's office. I was really upset, the principal said that he was disappointed that I had turned into a troublemaker. A letter to that effect was sent home with me.

The letter read, I was promptly accused of being a "trouble maker" and told that I would have to learn the American way of doing things. If I didn't succeed, I would be punished. My side of the story was never heard.

The following evening a group of kids followed me on my short cut home across a vacant lot. This time my persecutor was a different kid. His problem being that I didn't understand quite all that was being said but I had scored one hundred in arithmetic. Over the next week I turned into a real punching bag. I hit back a few times and hurt my hands. I really didn't like this fighting.

Usually I was dusty if not muddy, by the time I arrived home. Aunt Mitch told me that I better learn to fight back; that was "the American way". I wanted so much to be a good American and I wanted her to be pleased with me. I just didn't understand some of the requirements needed, to become a good citizen.

Ann Carpenter, a cute blonde and I hit it off pretty well. She invited me to parties where I learned to play games called "spin the bottle" and "post office". America was really a neat place! After a few days I walked her home, there, I met her older brother Dick. He was familiar with my predicament, he said that he had heard about it and that all the boys in the fifth grade were going to take turns beating up the French kid. I asked him what I had done, he said "nothing, you're just different".

He was in the eighth grade and had been through his share of fights. We went to his garage where he started coaching me on covering up and several other basic skills. His most important bit of advice was "get the first punch in and don't ever give up, just keep punching".

Monday came quickly; we studied Egyptian history. I copied the alphabet in hieroglyphics and promptly sent a note to my friend Ann. That afternoon was the turn of one of the class bullies; he was heavier and taller than the rest. He had a habit of taking money from the fourth graders by threatening to beat them up. Before we squared off he began taunting me. I didn't say anything, I walked up to him and punched him in the mouth as hard as I could. He fell back and started crying. There was a second of absolute silence then everybody in the circle cheered. He got up and left. The same thing happened a couple more times once with a sixth grader. Within two or three days my fights were over. Soon I was elected president of my class. I thought again about "knocking on the dragon's door" My theory had been reinforced.

I don't think that I ever had the chance to thank Dick.

Thanks Dick!

Bobby Daniels, a classmate who lived across the street offered to let me ride his bicycle. It had been several months since I had ridden one in France, so happily I mounted and started riding up Third Street. The street between Lighthouse and Central Avenue was pretty steep. I pedaled up the hill with no problem and turned around to go back down. The bicycle and I gained momentum; I squeezed the handlebars looking for the brakes, there weren't any. I only had a half a block to go before the busy thoroughfare of Central Avenue. Bobby yelled, "use the brakes" to the top of his lungs. I looked again in vain for the brakes.

Speeding cars in either direction of Central gave me little hope of missing one, or of being missed. I imagined flattening myself on the open side of one of those Coca-Cola trucks. I spotted a tall hedge on the right and instinctively turned into it. It did its job. The bike and I both stopped. Actually the bike stopped, I continued over the handlebars into the fence behind the hedge. I was picking myself up rubbing the bump on my head and my bruised knee when Bobby ran down chastising me for not applying the brakes. I told him I tried but they weren't there. He looked really scared as he gave me a valuable lesson in the use of "Bendix" brakes.

Philip's father had the garage where all the newspaper boys in the area met to fold and pick up their papers for the afternoon routes. He offered me twenty-five cents an hour to fold and band papers. I went home and told my mother, so pleased! Kids in France didn't get paid for the jobs they did. Their food and lodging was pay enough. This time I had a job earning my own money.

Soon I had enough to open a savings account. Half of my earnings had to go into the account. One week I bought a gun belt and cap pistol, then a week later a cowboy hat. Saturday mornings Bobby and I would walk across town to go to the movie. For twenty-five cents we purchased a ticket that would let us in for two showings of Roy Rogers, Red Ryder, Hopalong Cassidy, Lash Larue and others. Of course there were the weekly serials to insure that we wouldn't miss a Saturday. For another twenty-five cents we bought a bag of popcorn and a soft drink. Full-length features like "Dick Tracy Meets Cue Ball" began to intermingle with the westerns taking some of my interest away from the Westerns. From time to time Ann met me at the movie; we sat together and held hands.

I had been taking my lunch to school in a brown paper bag like the majority of kids. I wanted a black lunch box with a thermos bottle in it. A couple of weeks of banding papers later, I decided that if I didn't put half of my earnings in the bank I had enough money. Full of apprehension I went to the dime store after the movies and bought the one I wanted. My apprehension was well founded. Though I came home proudly with the purchase I had made with my wages, Aunt Mitch grilled me. It seemed that she had deduced that I had used what should have been my savings. There was no sense in denying it. I told her that I had bought it to look more American like she wanted me to look. I guess I struck a chord. She did let me keep the lunch "pail" as she called it. In the future I would turn my earnings over to her and she would allow me half.

Uncle Russell and Aunt Mitch went back to Oregon so mother and I stayed in the house. It was almost like our own house minus bombs, fires and fear. I continued in school, by then I was pretty fluent in English. None of the courses had been changed to make it easier for me. If I was to live here I would have to learn to read and speak like everyone else. What a concept that was!

Dr. Fisher and his wife visited us quite often. He was the director of the Hopkins Marine Station who painted as a hobby. He decided that he would do a portrait of me. My mother agreed that I was to sit for him on Saturday mornings. He paid me twenty-five cents per hour. That seemed to be my going rate.

The time that he wasn't painting Dr. Fisher spent with a pet pelican. We carried his cage to the beach where he released him after having tied a cat collar tightly around his neck. To the collar he attached a strong fishing line that he could reel in with the largest reel that I had ever seen. It was mounted on a cut off fishing pole. The pelican caught fish but could not swallow it. Dr. Fisher reeled him in to take the fish out of his pouch. He then measured each one and categorized it. I wrote the results on ruled paper on a clipboard. Each trip to the beach he eased the collar enough for the pelican to be rewarded with one or two of his catch. He repeated the process four or five times before going back in.

A month or so later mother received a letter from Aunt Mitch telling her that it was time she found a job. Mother was distressed because she was really ill, on the verge of a nervous breakdown. She had been working hard trying to get Serge to join us. She made several trips by train to the French consul, I think in San Francisco. She had written numerous letters to the State Department all answers were the same, we would have to wait. Everybody was working on it, "those things took time."

She went on interview after interview for secretarial positions; she was very fast at short hand in French but not fast enough in English shorthand. In a few weeks she did find a job as a dental assistant. Our days fell into a pleasant routine.

Uncle Russell and Aunt Mitch came back for the summer vacation. Uncle Russell spent much of his time at the marine station doing research on sandollars and sea urchins. He took me with him daily. After watching him for a few days he showed me how to use a microscope and to start my own experiments on the division of egg cells. My interest grew and we began a daily ritual of observing the progress of fertilized eggs.

A friend of his, Dr. Spence, a retired rubber chemist, invited us to his house in the Seventeen Mile Drive of Pebble Beach, to show me some of his experiments with dyes and the color of rubber. We all went one Saturday to the beautiful Spanish styled house. He was very quick to tell us that he lived two doors down from somebody named Bing Crosby. I had never heard of the man.

Dr. Spence seemed to take a very deep interest in my mother and me. He would often come pick us up to go to lunch at Del Monte Lodge. Then we walked around the golf course with him while he played. I spent many hours at his house playing with his dog while he and my mother went into another room to discuss business.

Weekends passed quickly, I seldom went to the movies during the summer. We climbed into the old Nash and drove to many of the tourist attractions. Seal Rock, Cypress points, the Carmel Mission and even the lettuce farms of the Salinas valley. We even took a ride to a place where they attached a bumper placard showing a black circle with print that said the "Black Spot". We walked on flat ground but had to lean forward or maybe back. Every two weeks or so we picnicked in the Carmel valley at the Culp ranch. Mrs. Culp was a French war bride of World War I.

We were introduced to the Dufours, a woman, her mother and her daughter who lived in Carmel. The daughter had a hobby and toy store. I really enjoyed the time there.

Uncle Russell and I spoke of my father fairly often. He assured me that he would not try to replace him, but he would be glad to do some of the things that he and I might have done. Each weeknight we walked ten blocks or so to an ice cream parlor to buy a five-cent cone of a different flavor. Some nights we even had a ten-cent cone made up of two flavors. He said we had to be sure it was always gone by the time we arrived back at the house.

Mother and Aunt Mitch didn't seem to enjoy each other's company any more now than at Christmas. I had to hope that it would be all right.

At the end of June we drove to San Juan Bautista for the Fiesta and Rodeo. I wore my finest western gear, including hat and studded pistol belt. We attended the most fascinating event that I had ever seen, a real western rodeo, which took my undivided attention and enthusiasm. My pleasure was so apparent that the "Salinas Californian" used a picture of me for the cover of their bi-monthly magazine supplement along with a short article.

Almost a year after we arrived in this country, we received a call from Serge. He had just landed in New York and would be on his way the next day. We could hardly contain ourselves with the excitement we felt. At last our little family would be reunited.

We drove to San Francisco to meet him. We waited at the track where the train pulled into the station. Climbing into the nearest car, we asked the conductor if there was a French boy on the train and where he might be. He replied with a broad smile, "you mean Serge? Just keep going that way!" we half walked, half ran through the train, dodging passengers. Soon we heard him speaking English with a heavy French accent.

He had grown taller but he was even thinner than he had been. He had matured and he almost needed a shave. We all hugged, mother stepped back and looked at him, saying that she had lost a boy but had now gained a man as her son.

Serge turned to me asking if I had gotten used to this country and if I liked it. I assured him that France would never be forgotten but this was now my country. I had worked hard this first year trying to be a true American. Now when I placed my hand over my heart to recite the pledge to the flag of the United States, I knew that I was speaking of my country.

We both remembered what the symbol of this flag meant to us. Our freedom and our ability to be here to speak about it was due to the support of Americans soldiers as they followed their flag throughout France on their way to other countries of Europe, until the end of the war.

Serge and I spoke on the way to Pacific Grove. I told him what Aunt Mitch had said. She may have been right, "we had to learn the lesson of forgiveness for the past, to be tolerant of what had happened to my father and hundreds of thousands like him". I told Serge I was working on it but I had not yet grown spiritually to that extent. I still missed my father and I was still mad at the Germans for taking him away from us. Maybe he would be able to forgive faster than me since it was not his real father.

Journey Seven

Pacific Grove, California
to Lancaster, New Hampshire

Chapter Eighteen

Serge had been with us almost a week when he asked about school. He had played the piano in the house several hours each day but he needed to catch up with his math that had always been a little weak. Uncle Russell told him that in just a few days they would return to Portland and he would attend the University there.

One Sunday morning, Aunt Mitch told us to prepare for an all day trip to Palo Alto. We were to visit acquaintances for Sunday dinner. Mother told her that she preferred not to ride the hundred miles each way to visit someone she did not know and for whom she had no particular feeling. That seemed a bit extravagant and really pointless. It had been almost a year since we had experienced privations but it was still very real in our minds. To go that far for fun and a meal seemed a bit superfluous. There were still so many people in the world that we knew, who suffered from malnutrition and unacceptable lodging. Aunt Mitch became angry; the fact that her authority had been challenged was a bit unusual and difficult for her to accept. We were still grateful for the nice home that had been made available to us so rather than cause more hard feelings, we went.

During the trip we were told that the doctor we were to visit was a professor at Stanford University. His wife was writing a paper on civilian World War II survivors. We were cautioned to be tolerant of her questions and to answer them as completely as possible. Mother became furious, " We are not specimens to be exhibited as in a sideshow, just stop and let us out, we will find our way back!"

Uncle Russell in his patient tone worked hard to smooth things over, successfully I might add. We made the visit, had a good meal but were not asked any questions.

The trip back was not pleasant, Aunt Mitch lectured us on the strengths of this country, on the fact that we were free and would always be free because of their generosity. There was no threat of danger in this country, it's might sent chills of fear to citizens of every other country in the world.

We felt that we really understood those things better. We had just seen that might challenged by Germany and we had read about it being challenged by Japan, unsuccessfully, but still challenged. It would happen again.

That night we had a small family meeting in mother's room. Serge would go to Portland in just a few days. Mother said that she was getting sicker by the day. It was mostly nerves, and mental anguish. She could never become the non-caring, scatterbrain that Aunt Mitch seemed to want her to be. Still she didn't want to seem ungrateful, but to keep her sanity we would have to do something different. I could see that the situation would not improve so I suggested that we telephone Wayne in New Hampshire. I remembered something he had told me when we were there. " Any time that you and your mother are in trouble let me know. I will help any way I can. I don't have much but I will help". Her face seemed to light up. I knew that was what she really wanted. I would have preferred Connecticut with Uncle Abe but my turn would come. "We will go call him right away," she said, and she did, not thinking that it was four hours later there.

Wayne answered the telephone almost immediately. He sounded very glad to hear from us. He listened quietly, seldom interjecting any words of his own. After listening to our idea he said that he had an old house on a hill in the middle of five uncultivated acres. The house needed repairs but he could start on it right away to make it livable. We were welcome to it as long as we wanted it and he would call us back when it would be comfortable enough to live in.

The next morning mother sent me out to play with Bobby while she told the Moores of her plans. I came in for lunch to a very quiet kitchen. I didn't find out what was said until four years later.

Less than a week had passed when we heard from Wayne. The house was not finished but it was livable. Mother went to the railroad station to buy our tickets. We packed our bags the next day and left that afternoon.

We said our good-byes, Aunt Mitch looked at me with tears in her eyes, her lips were very pale and her mouth was clenched into a straight line. She did not offer to take us to the train so mother called a taxi. Aunt Mitch's repeated concern about our ability to make our own way in this country was not well founded. The trip to Boston was long and uneventful. I spoke English fluently with hardly a trace of a French accent. We found the next train to Lancaster with little trouble. Wayne met us at the station. Already it was cold on the first of October. We arrived shortly after Wayne's birthday. He said our coming was his birthday present.

The drive to our new home was almost ten miles. Wayne had hot soup waiting for us on the back of the enameled, wood burning stove. The two-story house was in different stages of completion. The upstairs bedrooms looked almost finished, only the "Celotex" walls needed painting. The house was a far cry from the luxurious house of Uncle Abe and the quaint comfortable house of Uncle Russell. But we could have had a lot less. In fact we could have been dead.

Thoughts like that always came to my mind when I felt a little less than thankful for the material things that we had.

As soon as we had settled down, Wayne showed us where the "Grange" school was, two and a half miles away. I was registered in the sixth grade of the one room schoolhouse. Mrs. Rogers was fortunate enough to have students in a complete range of grades from first to eighth. The sixth grade had four students, Pricilla and another boy and girl. The seventh grade had four also and the eighth had two.

Mrs. Rogers was a strict disciplinarian who devoted most of her attention to the lower grades and expected the upper grades to be self-motivated. She was a patient person who was capable of shifting from "Dick and Jane" to algebra in the same sentence. The burden was on the classes that had to determine which group she was addressing.

Wayne was very pleased that I was there. He had no children but said that we would do many things together. He had a poultry house with two thousand laying hens. Each morning before school and afternoons after school I had the privilege of gathering eggs. After supper Wayne and I went down to the unheated basement to grade and box the day's productions. He had selected the poultry business because the dairy business required that cows be milked twice a day. This to me however, was almost as demanding.

New England farm life allowed very little free time. I learned how to chop enough wood each day to satisfy the appetite of the ravenous stove. Not only was it used to cook and to heat the downstairs; it provided hot water through heating coils in the firebox.

Wayne had been a hunter and trapper earlier in his life. Fox pelts brought fifteen or twenty dollars each. So he ordered animal traps from one of the mail order catalogues. He showed me how and where to set the traps with the hope of catching foxes. Any pelt I was able to sell we would split fifty-fifty. That seemed even better than the twenty-five cents per hour I had been earning.

Chickens are not the smartest of nature's creatures. In the morning there were usually one or two dead hens in corners, having either smothered or frozen to death. One was dressed for the pot, the other I used as bait for my traps.

My first memorable catch was on a school morning. At daylight after having completed my chores Wayne told me to check my traps, he thought I had caught something. I went to the pile of old tin roofing under which I had set two traps. I saw movement, curiosity getting the better of me, I eased closer to peek under the tin. I met a skunk for the first time. I ran to the house, the stench seemed to get worse until I realized I was using my polluted hand to cover my nostrils. I reached the woodshed door just as Wayne opened it laughing. He told me to take my clothes off as he handed me a towel to wrap in until I could get to the tub. He mixed vinegar, Epsom salts and molasses and tomato juice in the bath water. Then I had to rinse off the mixture with cold water. He said it would help get rid of the smell.

I was late for school so I left the skunk where it was, Wayne said that he would shoot it to take it out of it's misery, but he would leave it to me for disposal. Apparently I still had an aura, because the instant that I walked into school I was asked to go back home. That afternoon, Johnny Alden stopped on his way home offering to help me dispose of the carcass. I picked an old feed sack, tied a bandanna around my face as I had seen highwayman do in western movies and waited for Johnny to come back. I thought he had gone home to change clothes, but he came back with his father's pickup truck.

I had planned on taking the skunk deeper into the woods but he said no, he had a better idea. We placed the dead skunk in the sack and drove to the Grange school. The old building was raised off the ground, allowing us to snake on our stomachs to the middle of the school, almost under the potbellied stove. There we dumped the sack. School was canceled the next two days until Mrs. Rogers' husband removed the carcass. It was easy for him to see that the skunk had been shot, so it didn't take much to deduce who the culprit was, particularly after having been sent home for my less than pleasant aroma. For punishment, my Christmas present, a single shot .22 rifle was withheld for a full month.

I really was not a troublemaker but maybe in my eagerness to please I was easily swayed. This last escapade and smoking the cigarettes, both following other people's advice, got me in trouble. I didn't like being in trouble! I had learned the lesson earlier aboard the fishing boat, that since one was responsible for his actions he had to accept the consequences. This premise had been reinforced several times since, so I decided that I would no longer be a follower. How could I become a leader?

Leadership was not inborn, but I worked on it. Whether my religious years at Siecq and in school with the nuns had anything to do with the development of my own sense of ethics I'm not sure. Regardless of the cause, it cost me friends. I wasn't one of the guys. I wouldn't go with the others to turn over outhouses or to let the air out of the teacher's tires.

I spoke English fluently but still with a very slight accent. This made me the object of several pranks. One sub zero day in January, Johnny told me how great the frost on top of a milk can tasted. Innocently, I bent over and licked the can top. My tongue promptly stuck to it. They all laughed. A good five minutes later I was still stuck. One of my "friends" knocked the lid loose and Priscilla helped me carry it inside the house to run water on it. They may have been reprimanded, but I doubt it; even the adults thought it was funny. Later when I got over being mad, I figured out that anyone should have known better than to do such a stupid thing. Then I thought it was pretty funny too.

I never did catch a fox, but really I didn't mind. Seeing that skunk captive, frantically thrashing around with his leg in a trap made me think again of how my father and millions of people like him must have felt in concentration camps. I have since, never liked zoos with cages and would only take my children to the more modern types with the natural habitat.

The weekly radio programs such as the Lone Ranger and Jack Benny entertained us. The rest of my time was spent in the chicken house or chopping wood.

Mother was now working as a bookkeeper for a drug company. She drove the old 1939 Ford in the snow every day. The winter of 1948 was one of the coldest on record. The temperature dipped to fifty-two degrees below zero for two or three days. Only two thermometers in town could register that low. School was canceled and we left the house just to feed the hens and refill the kerosene heaters. I developed pneumonia but fortunately we had access to a doctor with sulfa drugs. In a relatively short time I was back at school.

Spring came and I was told to plant a strawberry patch. I was given a half-acre to cultivate and fertilize with chicken manure. I think the weeds grew a lot faster than the strawberries. I spent time every day hoeing the weeds.

The school year ended and I had done well. The Alden kids and I spent a few hours a week at a lake camp, fishing and learning to swim. I tried to get the other kids to help me with the hoeing but they were too busy. I had read "Tom Sawyer", it had been so easy to have his fence whitewashed, that I thought surely I could do the same. So much for my leadership skills! My strawberries were a flop and I was severely criticized.

Mother and Wayne called me in one Saturday. This was the first time that I had seen Wayne in a suit. Mother still had nice clothes from France so it was not unusual to see her well dressed. They told me to go take a bath and get dressed we were going to town for them to be married.

I was in shock. They had never even hinted at the possibility of marriage. Mother and I were quite certain that my father would never return from the concentration camp, in fact we felt that he was no longer alive, but I still hoped. Surely mother knew that getting married meant she had given up all hope. I went to take my bath, this time I cried.

Sure, Wayne was all right but I had never considered that he might become my new father. We got along fine, but I had no real affection for him.

I wondered if my mother was doing this out of gratitude or if she really felt that he could make a good and loving husband. I wanted her to be happy but I had never seen any sign of affection from him toward her. He was nothing like my father had been. He had started spending more time at the house. Surely, she could have told me something was brewing. In the last few months we had not spoken and shared our thoughts as we had in California. There, I had been somewhat the man of the house. Here, my position had been usurped and I was just a kid who seemed to be in the way.

We drove to town in silence. The marriage was held in the Methodist parsonage instead of a church. Only mother's boss, his wife and daughter Mary and I were there. Mother cried, I didn't know if they were tears of sadness or of joy. I thought probably sadness.

I had been to weddings in France. In fact I had been one of the altar boys at several. They were always held in church, even when older people were married. There, everyone seemed very happy, shouting congratulations to the bride and groom. I didn't even know that you could be married as they were. The mayor of the town married those in France who couldn't be married in the church. I had never attended a Methodist church and knew nothing about them. In fact since we had moved to Lancaster we had not gone to any church. I felt let down, for as far back as I could remember I had always gone to mass on Sunday, sometimes, even when I was sick. While in California, I walked to church by myself, but still I went.

The brief ceremony over, we went to Mr. and Mrs. Lund's house for dinner. Then, I was told that I had been invited to spend the night. Wayne would bring my pajamas and clothes for the next day. I spent the night upstairs in Mary's brother's room. He was away at college.

Mary also attended the Grange school. She was a year older than me and had a boyfriend, so we had not spoken very much. There seemed to be a tremendous age gap between a seventh grade girl and a sixth grade boy. That night we made up for the previous year. Her room was also upstairs while her parent's room was downstairs.

I had left my door partially open. I lay awake wondering what this new development would mean to our family. Serge was doing well in college so he would stay in Portland for another year. I wondered if he had been told of this impending marriage. I would have to write to him.

Mentally I prepared myself for more of the Grange school and work on the chicken farm.

Mary waited until after her parents had gone to bed; she came in wearing flannel pajamas. She whispered, asking if I was awake? She plopped on my bed, as I said "yes", not sure of what to expect. She said simply "Do you want to talk?" I sat up and we talked for at least two hours. Actually, I listened most of the time. Her parents didn't get along. Her father thought he was in love with my mother and her mother knew it. What would I do now that she and Wayne were married? Mary really didn't want to go to high school in Lancaster. She could go live with an aunt in Massachusetts, but her father was an important man in town so it would be better if she stayed.

Mary began to cry. I felt she must have had deeper problems than the ones she had already voiced. I held out my hand hesitantly, she took it and held on tight. Shortly, she stopped crying saying she was getting cold. She told me to move over, climbed in bed with me and pulled the covers up. Her mother woke us up in the morning, screaming at us. She called Mary a few names and told me to get dressed and out of the house and to never come back. Her father had already gone to work and was not aware of our predicament. Mary tried to explain that it had been very innocent, we had been talking and just went to sleep. Nothing she said was heard and the tirade continued.

That was probably the biggest mistake Mary's mother could have made. By the first of May she had started working in the store with her husband to keep track of him so maman said. Mary began to ride her bicycle to the creek where we met at a swimming hole. As soon as I finished my chores I would tell mother I was going swimming. We became extremely good friends throughout the summer. Mary's boyfriend seemed to have been forgotten.

His interests lay in calves and tractors, besides he lived about the same distance from school as we did but in the opposite direction.

We spent hours swimming in our underwear, then drying off in the sun. We spoke of the future; she wanted to be a pediatrician. I wanted to be a diplomat. I was almost thirteen and she was just fourteen. We had our marriage plans all made. We still had high school and college but all that would go fast and we would be together always.

Toward the end of summer, she and I were drying under a big maple tree, both of us only wearing briefs when Johnny and his little brother Peter came to swim. We grabbed for our clothes, but a bit late. The boys razzed us a little. We dressed and left. Regretfully, it didn't end there. The boys told their sister Pricilla, who told her mother, who in turn told Mary's mother and mine. Two weeks later mother received a letter from the Moores saying that they would be glad to have me stay with them.

Apparently mother had written them about my escapade with Mary, saying that her father wanted me out of the region. This was not good! I was not even thirteen and I was being run out of town. I walked the distance to Mary's house traveling through the woods instead of the road. There I waited until I saw her near her window. I threw a handful of gravel against the glass and got her attention. We met briefly one more time, she already knew that I was to leave. We kissed several times and told each other we would wait forever. I never saw her, again!

The following week, Wayne drove us to Boston, where I boarded a train for Oregon he seemed more jovial than usual. I was back to traveling alone again. I was really looking forward to it. I imagined that I was on an adventure that would bring me to untold riches. The train took the northern route through Chicago, Cedar Rapids then close enough to Mt. Rushmore for us to see the presidents. A lady who had me sit with her, adopted me for the trip. At different times, she told a few men who seemed to be bothering her that I was her son, so they left her alone. It was a good deal for both of us. I told her that I was never allowed to have comic books, neither by the Moores nor at home, so she bought me a dozen. I read them, then she read them.

There was a problem with the train in Boise, Idaho. We had to get off for a few hours. We left the station to find a restaurant to eat supper. I hesitated going with her, but I had very little money with me and I was hungry. Throwing advice and caution to the wind I went with her. Nothing happened, we had a good meal and made it back to the train in time for departure.

Uncle Russell, Aunt Mitch and Serge met me at the station in Portland. I had finished another journey safely.

Journey Eight

Lancaster, New Hampshire
to Portland, Oregon

Chapter Nineteen

We arrived at 4714 North Amherst. It was a neat, one story, two bedroom home, close to Uncle Russell's work at the Portland University. He pointed out that the streets in that area were all named after well-known universities. My room was the one in the back with corner windows, small but comfortable with what looked like new furniture.

I spoke to Serge about our mother's marriage to Wayne as soon as we were alone. He had just found out by letter two days before. Surprisingly, he really didn't seem to care. That shocked me, but then I started thinking that he had gone through what I was experiencing when our mother divorced his father and married mine.

I never knew exactly what kind of relationship Serge had with his father who had left Paris for Algeria when Serge was four. He had been a better than average painter with a tremendous wanderlust, who admired Paul Gauguin enough to try to emulate parts of his life.

The next day we went to the Portsmouth Elementary School, only a few blocks away from my new home. I had my sixth grade report card and was registered in the seventh grade.

In the next two days Aunt Mitch laid out the ground rules. I was to walk to school, come home and do my homework. Aunt Mitch would then teach me Latin four days a week after my schoolwork. My allowance would be twenty-five cents per week. Every other Saturday I would cut the grass for twenty-five cents for the front and twenty-five for the back. I could either listen to two, half hour programs before supper or a one hour after. Saturday morning I could listen to "Let's Pretend". Saturday afternoon I was encouraged to listen to the "Texaco" sponsored "Saturday at the Opera". I should be able to read at least two books per week in the same categories as Kippling's "Jungle Books" and Mark Twain's classics. Comic books would not be allowed in the home.

My duties would consist of making my bed, keeping my room clean, drying dishes and taking out the garbage. I could go to the movies once per month if I had kept enough money to pay for it. I could make two five-minute telephone calls per day to boys, unless it was pertaining to schoolwork. Did I have any questions?

For my birthday Uncle Russell gave me a great stamp album. I was allowed to indulge in this new hobby without any restrictions as long as my compulsories were completed.

My grades remained in the "A" category except for an occasional "B" in history for which I received extended counseling.

Serge lived on campus during the week. Weekends he came to the house and slept on the living room sofa.

Aunt Mitch was originally from North Carolina and Uncle Russell from Nebraska. She graduated with honors from Bryn Mawr. Each had a PHD, I really don't remember from which university, she in chemistry, he in biology. I had the privilege of being reminded almost daily of those accomplishments. She was a good cook and an excellent homemaker.

The first few months, I wrote my mother almost every two weeks. Perhaps once a month I received a return letter from her, with the obligatory "take care" from Wayne. As the year progressed, the frequency decreased.

In the spring I joined troop "86" of the Boy Scouts. Quickly I became assistant patrol leader. At last, I was on my way to elementary leadership.

That pretty much summed up my year in the seventh grade. At the end of school we closed up the house and went to Pacific Grove for the summer.

Aunt Mitch and I had planned for that, weeks in advance. The first three weeks I would go to the Boy Scout Camp Meriwether, named after Meriwether Lewis. I entered several competitions, and came in second for the two-twenty yard dash. But I won the first place medal for all age groups in the marksmanship competition. Camp finished, I took a Greyhound bus down the Pacific Coast Highway to "PG" as it was called.

Uncle Russell and I were to go daily to the Hopkins Marine Station to conduct and record further experiments. Afternoons, I continued my Latin lessons. We didn't want my "brain to turn to mush".

I met Jim, who was my age. We hit it off and started camping in the Carmel Valley almost every other week. We acquired two halves of an army surplus "pup tent" and some old quilts. We brought along his "portable" radio. The batteries alone must have weighed over five pounds. When the tent was dark we listened to "The Shadow", and "Inner Sanctum" then cringed at every sound of nature until we slept.

Jim introduced me to his two pet king snakes. They were large enough that, coiled around each arm they went from wrist past his elbows. His supreme thrill was to take them to the movies and release them close to a group of girls. He of course claimed that they escaped. He would have to get on his hands and knees to retrieve them amid screams of terror or maybe mock terror. He said it was much better than mirrors on his shoes.

He let me borrow one of the snakes one night. I had no particular plan for it but I proudly showed it to Aunt Mitch. Though she thought herself to be somewhat of a naturalist she and snakes were not on the best of terms. I found myself in the back of the old Nash, snake in a small laundry bag safely locked in the trunk, on our way back to Jim's house.

Later that summer he and I ran into a diamond back rattler on one of our trips. I found no reason to be afraid, but I did learn to balance on a fence post until the snake grew bored and moved on.

The experiments went well in the laboratory. Uncle Russell taught me the basics of microphotography. Then I learned an even more valuable lesson. Uncle Russell was applying various solutions to fertilized sea urchin eggs to record their effects on film. I went to his worktable and started smelling the bottles. One really smelled good, it reminded me of almonds. I took a second deep whiff and collapsed to my knees. I had enough presence of mind to call out and set the bottle on the table. Fortunately it was only a dilute solution of potassium cyanide. Uncle Russell eventually regained his composure, he then explained patiently that one should never smell the contents of a bottle. "You remove the stopper, then smell only the stopper. Some solutions in a laboratory can be deadly".

The Moores did a lot to round out my education during my eighth grade year. We visited "Cannery Row" of Steinbeck Fame in New Monterey. We drove to San Francisco to see a Benvenuto Cellini exhibit on our way back to Oregon. We attended three days of a week long

Shakespeare festival in Bend, Oregon. We fed the chipmunks on nature trips to Crater Lake. We held annual season tickets to the symphony and ballet. We also went to see "The Tempest", "Harvey" and a seasons worth of other stage plays.

The eighth grade was challenged with a declaration that we would accelerate my Latin lessons so that I could spend an hour a day learning to play the piano. Aunt Mitch told me that it just didn't make sense that Serge was pursuing an advanced degree in music and I didn't even play the piano. I told Aunt Mitch that my father had planned on teaching me the violin, the instrument that most Hungarian boys were expected to master. She, in her inimitable way, told me that since my father was not taking care of my education she would do what she thought best for me. Furthermore, she could teach me the piano but not the violin.

One Saturday after the beginning of school I went to the community swimming pool. I stood on my heels in the gutter edge, looking down. One of the smaller kids ran by giving me a shove. I pushed off and somehow knocked myself out. Everyone thought I was playing. Finaly I woke up, with blood all around me in the water. Someone did realize that I had a problem and pulled me out.

My interest in members of the opposite sex was growing. I was debating between two lovely young misses, one blonde and the other a brunette when another girl came on the scene. She made her interest known by dropping a flower "frog" onto my chair, the kind with several dozen very sharp spines used in flower arrangements. I felt certain that she meant to cause only slight discomfort and probably would have, had I sat down like a right and proper young man. Unfortunately boys of that age don't really sit, at least I didn't. When I finished answering a question in English class, I flopped down, jamming several dozen spikes through my jeans. I let out a yelp, stood up and gingerly pulled the object symbolizing her interests from my behind.

At that time I received a quick lesson comparing the much more expedient system of accusation, verdict and sentencing to perhaps expending a little time in fact finding that could, heaven forbid, develop into some kind of system called, justice in schools. I was the one sent to the principal's office for disrupting the class, blood running down my leg, starting to saturate my jeans enough to bring the class down in uproarious laughter. Later Rosemarie reinforced her declaration of affection by kicking me in the shins at the bus stop.

The Moores had decided to adopt me. Whether it was for personal reasons or tax purposes I never knew. My mother approved with a statement, "that is, if it was all right with me". A big push was made to win my agreement. My allowance was doubled to fifty cents a week and I was allowed to listen to an additional half-hour of radio daily.

I had almost a week to make up my mind before the prearranged court date. I spent hours wondering what I may have done to displease my mother so, for her to be so willing to abandon me to this older couple. It didn't make sense! She had worked so hard and spent a lot of money to save me from the Gestapo, then to bring me to America. Of course there was also the request from my father that she promise to do everything she could for us to remain together regardless of his destiny. I was accustomed to living with other families, but then, there had been good reasons.

I was crushed, since she had not even corresponded with me to discuss this possibility. It had to have something to do with her new husband.

We had endured many hard months during the German occupation. I had lost my father and she her husband. True we had not been together for most of the time since my sixth birthday, but the circumstances made it acceptable. Now, we were in a free country that mother had felt held our future together, but now she made the decision for us to be separated. I hoped that she only wanted to give me a chance at the best education available, but I also felt that being together was part of my education.

I went to see Serge in his dormitory to ask his opinion and advice. He began to tell me about a set of Norwegian twins he was dating, he wasn't sure which of the two he was in love with. They had introduced him to a new wonderful dish called "lutefisk". As an afterthought feeling compelled to answer my questions he told me to do what I wanted. He would be graduating at the end of the year and had been accepted by the Eastman School of Music to work on his Master's Degree, so he would be moving to Rochester.

I laid awake for two nights planning my trip back to New Hampshire. I went as far as the Greyhound bus station to inquire about fares to Boston. I thought that if I made it there they would see what a great kid I was, and certainly they wouldn't force me to come all the way back to Oregon. Unfortunately I had saved only enough money for a bus ticket part way to Chicago. I knew that anything I did had to be done before we went to court.

The second night I had a long, one way conversation with my father. I asked his advice; whether he was ever coming back, and if he missed me as much as I missed him. Then, frustration took over since he was unable to answer me. I got mad at the Germans for taking him from us, but mostly from me. I cried myself to sleep.

My decision came finally during the third night of deliberation. It had become quite simple. The Moores were the only people who were showing an interest in me at all, regardless of the reason. At breakfast I told Uncle Russell and Aunt Mitch that I agreed! Aunt Mitch cried, I guessed with joy. That was really one of the few signs of affection that I ever saw from her. Maybe I wasn't sensitive enough then, to realize that the time and effort she spent with my supplemental education was the only way that she could show affection.

I didn't have to meet with anyone prior to our appearance in court. Though I was innocent of any crime, I felt extremely small and certainly cowered by the judge looking down at me from his elevated bench. Sagely, he asked if I had made this decision of my own free will? I told him that I had. He then asked if I wanted to change my name to Moore? I panicked, that question had not come up. I wanted to please them to show that I was grateful, but also I recalled a conversation my father and I had, when he told me that I was the last Geller in our family.

I looked at the Moores and then at the judge. I told them that I realized that offering me their name was a special privilege and I was very thankful. However, I felt that I should honor my father and our family name, even though the name Geller may have been dangerous in Europe and probably had much to do in causing his arrest and probable death.

Again I thanked them, then said that I would prefer to keep my family name, hoping that someday I would have a son to carry the Geller name forward. The Moores agreed, I could tell reluctantly; but they nodded to the judge. The documents were signed and in a few strokes of the judge's pen I "belonged" to Dr. Russell and Mrs. Mary Mitchell Moore. I felt like I had been bought at a stock auction.

Serge came for Christmas dinner. He arrived while I was practicing the piano. He sat next to me and started critiquing; I'll just call it criticizing. I was holding my hands wrong, the tempo was off and I was playing kid stuff. I was old enough to play better. So I asked him how he was doing in Differential Calculus as I got up to leave. He slammed the cover down on the keys and got up too. That set the tone for the Christmas celebration. I received a bicycle from New Hampshire. All my friends had "Schwinn's"; I had a "Firestone Pilot". It wasn't as nice and didn't have a horn but I was still grateful, I no longer had to walk to school like the younger kids.

One of my neighbors was a freshman at Roosevelt High School where I was to attend classes the following year. Victor was having a very hard time with Latin. His parents asked me to help him. They paid me fifty cents an hour. My worth was finally going up. I soon found out his problem. He just really didn't want to study; all he did was talk. Somehow we managed to concentrate enough for him to catch up to the class and make a "C" at the end of the grading period. His father was so pleased that he gave me an extra ten dollars. I told Aunt Mitch that I would prefer tutoring to learning the piano. She seemed relieved saying, "well it's your choice".

The school year was nearing an end. The main topic of conversation was graduation gifts. They were anything from a bicycle to a trip to the Grand Canyon. Nothing had been said about a present for me. Really I thought that the diploma was what I had been working for. But kids came right out and asked what I was getting. I didn't want to seem different so I said it was to be a surprise. Their questions continued, so I went to the stationary store and bought myself a gray "Esterbrook" fountain pen. I took it to school saying that my mother had sent it. That seemed to satisfy the entire inquisitive bunch. I received my diploma along with a certificate for excellence. In the fall I would attend Roosevelt High School.

That year I didn't go to scout camp; instead the Moores accepted an invitation for me to spend a month with two of their lady friends who owned a house together in Lincoln Beach, on the Oregon coast.

I didn't understand the invitation since I had met them only once. I was assured that they were very interesting ladies since they were avid "rock hunters" and spelunkers. We loaded the car for the annual trip to Pacific Grove; we would simply detour through Astoria, go down the coast highway and drop me off in Lincoln Beach. I took my place in the back seat sharing it with Tatsu and Grover, the two black cats. Most of the trip they spent sunning themselves on top of the back window deck.

The two ladies, Sharon and Elizabeth welcomed us to the stilted house. The two had been together so many years that they looked almost like sisters. They certainly dressed alike in slacks and checkered shirts. Both were very pleasant and quick to serve tea and biscuits.
One hour later the Moores were on their way south.

The house had only one bedroom so I was assigned to the small closed in sun porch overlooking the Pacific. A stone polishing wheel, plumbed with a long rubber tube connected to the kitchen sink was mounted on a workbench in one corner of my porch. The kitchen was the usual seat of social gathering. The overstuffed living room chairs welcomed serious reading. Several hundred books lined one entire wall in a combination of built in and free standing bookshelves. Baskets full of polished agates and unusual crystal were scattered throughout the house.

I spent the first week there totally bored. I walked on the beach every afternoon looking in vain for anyone close to my age. The mornings were still too cold and windy. I looked for books that I might find interesting. There must have been a copy of every book ever published on rock hunting, stone polishing and spelunking. I pulled up a chair to reach the top shelf when I was told those books were not for me to read. I obeyed, but the seed had been planted. I would have to find a way to see what those books were about.

My hostesses took turns cooking. Sharon was the flapjack at breakfast, and soup and sandwich at lunch, specialist. Elizabeth was the supper expert. I wiped dishes. There was a debate over the evening glass of wine. Elizabeth felt that her evening meals would be much more enjoyable if served with a glass of wine. Sharon on the other hand said I was too young. It really didn't make any difference to me since I had been drinking watered down wine, in the French fashion for children, for at least ten years. They decided that watered wine was a viable compromise. White wine however is really not good diluted so it was agreed that I could drink a half a glass of white and a full glass of red diluted with a little water. I was amazed that such a minor proposition became such an important topic in the lives of my hostesses.

The tourist season didn't really start until after the fourth of July, even then, Lincoln Beach was not a Mecca for tourists. A few dozen high school kids went to the beach on picnics. Most groups were tucked away among the low sand dunes to facilitate their beer drinking, away from adult eyes.

There was no great mystique in beer to me, so I declined several invitations to join groups smoking and drinking. I was more interested in finding attractive girls. To date I had been unsuccessful; I met two sisters that didn't meet my qualifications, so I kept searching. I guessed that the search, like the chase to hunters, was my incentive.

I found Becky one afternoon during my third week of beach combing. I felt that a girl named Becky should be blond, however this one had long raven hair. She was sunbathing, reading a book. There was no one else on that part of the beach for a quarter mile in either direction. Without seeming too obvious, so I thought, I walked past her fifty yards turned around and passed her in the opposite direction. I did this, three or four times before she looked up and said hello. I took my cue from her greeting and joined her.

She sat up and began brushing her shiny black hair, guiding the brush with both hands. Her name was Rebecca, better suited to jet-black hair. She was from Corvallis and was spending the summer with her divorced aunt who worked during the day. She was going to be a sophomore in high school to my freshman year. She looked pretty mature and filled out her swim suit better than I could possibly have hoped. She didn't like to smoke and drink but she really liked to "neck". Her introduction complete, I looked to the heavens and silently said "Thank you, God!"

Aside from that, we did have similar intellectual interests, she was setting her sights on a law career and I still wanted to be in the diplomatic service. Other days I wanted to be a forest ranger or maybe a meteorologist. Diplomat sounded good though.

It took us less than a half-hour to tentatively investigate her favorite pastime. The first kiss was interrupted by a group of kids who conveniently started digging for clams fifty feet from us. Becky annoyed, stood up, handed me her beach bag, plucked her towel from the sand and said, "Let's go to my house".

Her wish, though not my command, was certainly my desire, so we went ten or twelve houses down from where I was staying. I asked why we had not seen each other before. She said she had only been there three days, had seen me walking on the beach and wanted us to meet. I thought it was wonderful. Here was a girl who knew what she wanted and was not restrained by the normal conventions of girlhood. She was more like a guy, she didn't play coy. It was more "this is what I want, let's get on with it".

Becky's weekends were spent with her aunt. I only had two left before my departure south. I wondered how I could extend my stay since my newfound friend and I seemed so *sympathique*, as we said in France.

The Saturday after my joyful meeting, my hostesses and I spent riding down the coast highway looking at rock formations and searching for agates. I found a black jasper, something that was not found too often. We went on south and visited sea lion caves. On the return trip we stopped in Depoe Bay to visit the aquarium. It had a great collection of sea anemones. We went immediately from there to the mineral museum, also in Depoe Bay. I was intrigued by a large piece of lodestone.

Sunday, Sharon and Elizabeth were invited to eat lunch with friends passing through. I simply had to warm leftovers for my lunch or fix a sandwich. It was a dreary, rainy day so I planned to stay in. Sharon had shown me how to use the wheel to polish stones so I would probably work on that or I might read. The ladies would be back within three hours.

I had thought about the books on that top shelf on several occasions. I stood on a stool and saw that the books were pretty dusty. If I moved them surely someone would be able to see traces. How was I going to look at least at one book? They seemed to be foreign.

One book was taller than the others, aside from that they were all set back about the same distance from the front of the shelf. I thought that if I used a table knife under the spine of the book using it as a bridge over the dust, I could use some type of hook to pull it from the shelf sliding it on the knife, without disturbing the dust. I worked for an eternity of five minutes and successfully extracted the book from its niche.

Carefully I opened the cover, it seemed almost new, and some of the pages had not yet been slit. My father had taught me to open a new book by opening it to the middle then, folding pages back on each side. I simply could not do this; I looked inside the partially opened pages. There was text on the left page and etchings on the right. They were of nude women in various stages and forms of embrace. There were enough words similar to French that I assumed the text to be in either Italian or Spanish. I quickly lost interest in the etchings and started the project of returning the book without leaving traces of my disobedience.

I must have been successful since no mention was ever made of the books. The ladies came back, perhaps a little tipsy, after their luncheon. Since I had learned that offense was the best defense I met them at the door with a stone that I had cut and polished to the size of a man's ring setting and asked them for a critique. I had been told that I would learn to make jewelry in shop the following year so I prepared for it.

That night I lay awake for hours anticipating my afternoon with Rebecca. She liked that name much better than Becky. I was to meet her on the beach right after lunch. I didn't think that I would tell her about the book yet. Maybe she would come over; I could get it down and we would look at it together.

Our usual flapjack breakfast finished I touched up a couple of places on my stone then looked at a new National Geographic Magazine. Around eleven I asked if I could eat lunch early, then headed for the beach with eager anticipation.

I didn't see anyone where we were to meet. It was still early, so I waded in one of the tidal pools trying to catch shrimp with my bare hands. Tiring of that quickly I found a place in the sand to sit and observe. Soon a young couple followed by a little boy walked along the edge of the water. Dad was closest to the lapping of the waves; son engrossed in his own pursuits constantly fell behind. Trying to catch up, he would run after his parents taking giant, jumping steps to land in his father's prints, before the ebbing waves washed away all evidence of his having been there.

I thought back a few years to the summer in La Flotte when I was five and we were a complete family. My mother and father had walked along the beach some seven thousand miles away, and I had done the exact same thing. I would fall behind skipping stones into the Atlantic, then run trying to catch up, also stepping in my father's eroding footsteps.

I looked further down the beach and saw a couple rolling around on the sand and I thought "soon that's going to be me". I waited for quite awhile; she still had not shown. Something must have happened, because surely Becky wouldn't be that late. We had really enjoyed the afternoon of innocent "smooching" at her aunt's house.

I decided to walk as far as the couple and back giving Becky a little more time. As I approached the writhing couple the tall blond guy appeared to be of college age. I smiled to myself thinking that you didn't have to be in college to do what he was doing. I glanced at his partner and froze. She was wearing a different swimsuit but she had the same raven hair. I turned around and ran. Pain, disappointment, anger, betrayal and nausea all flashed through me in seconds. Rebecca had said she liked to "neck", but it had only been three days since we agreed on the rendezvous. I slowed to a walk and headed back to the house. That was probably one of the most miserable days of my life.

Sharon, Elizabeth and I spoke of my trip to Pacific Grove. I had one more week; my bus was leaving the following Monday morning. I must have looked down in the dumps because that night the three of us went to the movie. After that we went to the "Twenty Flavors" and had a double ice cream cone.

That night I lay awake again, deploring my rejection of the morning. I was fed up with girls. I agreed with some of the older guys. You just couldn't trust them! I woke up early to a beautiful day and went to the beach right after breakfast. I made sure that I would not go in the direction of Becky's house. I didn't know why she wanted to be Rebecca anyway; Becky seemed fine to me.

I walked about a half a mile in the direction opposite my usual walks when I made the turn. Two little kids and a Collie ran by me on the nearly deserted beach yelling at "Lassie" to follow them. I continued my walk back toward the house glancing at the distant figure coming my way. The tide was out and I walked close to the water's edge. Occasionally, I picked up one of the few flat stones to skip it across the small incoming waves, thinking of the times Serge and I had done the same thing on *Ile de Ré*. I looked at cormorants fishing and didn't pay attention to the approaching figure.

She called my name as if nothing had happened. The explanation was simple. The blond guy was the son of one of her aunt's friends who was there for a long weekend. He was a freshman at Oregon State and she was just crazy about college guys. He was gone so we could take up where we left off.

"No, I didn't think so", I told her. I knew that we were not boy friend-girl friend but my pride dictated that I tell her that I was not an also ran. So I kept on walking. She turned around and headed back with me reaching for my hand. I didn't think it would hurt to hold hands while walking, but my resolve was there. We would not go back to the "necking " she liked so much.

We took a dip in a sun warmed tidal pool, then lay down on the sand to dry. In five minutes I had lost my resolve. At first I was firm, I didn't turn my head away but I kept my lips tightly pressed together. Then wonderful wonders, Rebecca smiling knowingly, eased the top of her bathing suit down to her waist. I had lost.

Monday came too quickly. Sharon and Elizabeth drove me to the bus stop close to the icehouse in Depoe Bay, where we said our good-byes. I boarded the bus around noon, then headed south on highway 101 for the next eight hundred fifty or so miles. They had given me a book for the trip. "Saddle Boys of the Rockies". It should probably have been interesting to a thirteen-year-old, but not to this one. I picked it up a half a dozen times and put it away each time. I was too busy reliving my last week.

Chapter Twenty

The trip south was uneventful, except for a runaway redwood logging truck with burned out brakes that tried to run down our bus. Our driver would have made Juan Fangio proud. He outran the truck for a good mile until he found an escape on a lookout, overlooking a beautiful valley. He slammed on the brakes, skidding to a stop just short of a three-foot stone retaining wall. The truck with only one gigantic redwood log went careening past us down the winding highway.

The screaming passengers settled down just long enough to give our driver a huge round of applause. He took his bow while sitting, by dousing his cap; he then backed us onto the highway to continue our trip. We passed the remains of our pursuer about a mile further down the hill. He had tried to slow against the side of the rocks, rolling the entire rig on its right side, sliding down the highway until he stopped. Fortunately the trailer and log had separated from the tractor and were jammed into the mountain. He was standing by the truck rubbing his shoulder, either a very skillful driver or a heck of a lucky fellow.

The bus arrived in San Francisco or Oakland and I had to change to another coach for Pacific Grove.

The rest of the summer was almost a carbon copy of the previous year. Uncle Russell and I did take a week to camp in the Big Basin National Park. We used my shelter half and Uncle Russell borrowed my friend Jim's so we could make a pup tent for shelter. The Forest Ranger warned us about leaving food out of metal containers. Bears were getting bolder and more accustomed to humans, they didn't hesitate to pilfer edibles, even in tents.

We met a man and his two sons who were doing the wilderness experience also. The first night after supper our newfound friends and we sat around a small campfire swapping stories and singing campfire songs. I watched one of the kids leaning back against his father's crossed legs, a smile of contentment on both of their faces. Then I looked at Uncle Russell, uncomfortable, sitting on the ground in old tweeds. He looked so out of place. His environment was really behind a lectern teaching physiology and history of science, or in a laboratory exited over the division of sea urchin and sand dollar eggs. I appreciated his efforts and felt warmth toward him for even trying to replace my father.

The songs over, and the plans for the next day made, the father emptied the dregs of his coffeepot drowning the glow of the remaining embers. We went to our tents. I took off my pants and rolled them for a pillow. It was a nice night so we left one of the tent flaps open. I lay in the Boy Scout sleeping bag that Uncle Russell had bought me the previous year, peering at the stars through leafy branches.

It had been several months since I had had more than a fleeting thought of my father. I was ashamed that my life was so comfortable that thoughts of my father were that far away. Years before, I had told myself that I would think of him at least once every day, and now I didn't even think of him once a week. That evening I wondered how he would do in this type of environment. He had always been in schools, offices, large hotels and large houses. Then I thought of what he had to endure in prisons and concentration camps. This probably would have been interesting to him and he would have written a story about our trip.

Summer over we went back to Portland. I was registered in the college preparatory curriculum at Roosevelt High School. The first gym class we had to run a few races, the hundred yard dash and a four-forty, then we had to sign up for a sport. The coach suggested I select cross-country in the fall and track in the spring.

I stayed out of mischief almost all year. I played baseball at Victor's house. Occasionally, the ball would land in an elderly widow's front yard. She would rush out of the house, yell at us and confiscate our ball. We got tired of that, so one day we walked to a bakery and looked at wedding cakes. We went back to Victor's house and telephoned the bakery. Victor fabricated the story his Aunt wanted to have a certain cake delivered to the grouch's address on a date that we knew we would be there to watch.

The bakery truck drove up and the delivery was made. There was a lot of gesticulating, the driver dropped off the cake on the doorstep and left. We thought we would really enjoy the feeling of winning, but it didn't turn out that way. The lady sat down on her threshold, head in hands crying. We didn't know why she cried. Maybe she didn't have the money to pay for it. We knew that she didn't have a car. Anyway the fun was gone out of the prank. Poor lady, we never did tell her where the order came from. We tried to justify our action, saying that she shouldn't take our balls, but that argument was pretty weak. So we didn't say anything, we rounded up ten dollars between us placed it in an envelope and dropped it in her mail slot when she wasn't there. That was another of those actions that one wonders about in later life.

School went very well, I took Spanish from Mrs. Richards. Since it was so close to French and I was on my third year of Latin, I thought that it would be a crib course. I was right. I was the only freshman with juniors and seniors. It turned out the cheerleading squad and the beauty court was in my class or I should say, I in theirs. I ended up tutoring almost a third of the upper-class beauties in school. I was the envy of the school's male population. That didn't set well with the guys on the football team, too bad!

I received a Christmas card from my mother and Wayne. There was no present that year. I sent them pictures but that was it.

Practice started for the track team. I made the freshman team in the mile and the three-quarter mile in the medley relay. One of the guys on the team was in my math, English and science classes. We finished our algebra pretty quickly, so two days a week Alex and I and two other students were allowed to sit in the back of the class and play chess. We scored pretty closely in our common subject. In track he could beat me in sprints but I always beat him in the mile.

I invited Alex to come to the house and do our homework together. He hesitated then said sure but he would have to call home from my house. We walked from the bus stop carrying our books. I opened the door and yelled to Aunt Mitch that I was home and had a guest. She came from the kitchen to meet him and I could see her freeze in mid step. I introduced them and showed him the phone. We went to my room, but it wasn't large enough for both of us to spread our books so we returned to the dining room. From where I sat I saw Aunt Mitch screw the mouth piece back on the telephone. Evidently she had washed and dried it. Alex stayed about an hour, we finished our homework and he said he had to go. I told him that I would see him the next day.

I was surprised; Aunt Mitch hadn't offered us a snack as she usually did. As soon as the door closed behind

Alex, Aunt Mitch sat down at the table. Her face was red and her hands were trembling. She started with a simple interrogation. How long had I known him? What did his parents do? And finally, why did I bring him home? It was uncomplicated in my mind, I said he was my friend. Then a side of that lady I never expected came out. She said with disdain, "but he is a Negro".

I was confused. Sure his skin was black and there were very few black students in that school, but he was a good guy and we were friends. That's all I needed to know. "Well in North Carolina, where she was from people respected each other's differences". I thought it was a quaint way to say that one had a stupid prejudice. The sum of that conversation was that he was no longer welcome in that house.

This was demoralizing; I was still getting over the German prejudices that were the cause of my father's probable murder. I thought that I was learning to be a good American, mostly by listening to Aunt Mitch. I couldn't believe that what I had just heard, was teaching me to be a good American. It hadn't been that long since she had told me to forget all that German "stuff".

I argued a bit, of course to no avail. Aunt Mitch was not accustomed to any questioning of her authority, not even by Uncle Russell. I was really disillusioned. Was this really the land of freedom? I knew I was a kid and therefore I didn't know everything and couldn't do everything I wanted, but this had to be something other than what we had journeyed so long and so far to find.

I asked what I was supposed to say to Alex the next day. She simply said, "That's up to you, just don't invite him". That night I wondered how I could stay in a house with someone who thought like that. The next school day Alex was quick to say that he would be unable to come back because that made him get home too late to do his chores. Whether that was true or whether he had sensed the tenseness of the atmosphere, I didn't know. We remained friends at school and at track meets.

During Easter vacation Uncle Russell had a chance to do some research at an oceanographic station in Friday Harbor, on San Juan Island in Puget Sound. He and I boarded a bus to Seattle where we spent the night at the St. Andrews Hotel. The next morning we took another bus to Anacortes where we boarded a ferry for San Juan Island. We registered in a smelly little hotel in Friday Harbor; we took one room with twin beds and a hot plate.

Uncle Russell became engrossed in his work and I went around the harbor looking at all type of flowers and stones. I borrowed a rowboat, and the daughter of the oceanographer who invited us went with me to a small island in the harbor. We spent one afternoon exploring the entire island before rowing back. One rainy day we stayed at their house listening to music. She was a great Gilbert and Sullivan fan.

Uncle Russell and I took the bus back to Seattle and another one back to Portland. The second leg was when I asked him about his views on Alex and people like him. He gave me an answer about respecting a man for his ability and achievements. So I asked why Aunt Mitch thought the way she did. He quickly said, "that", and religion were two topics he never discussed. All at once I was ashamed that people, especially educated people thought like that. But what could this thirteen-year-old do? I was now adopted; these were my folks, not my parents, but my folks.

Before we reached Portland I had decided that I would like to go to New Hampshire to visit my mother for a month in the summer. I thought to myself that maybe things had changed and that I would be more welcome. Then it would allow me to start working on leaving the Moores. I mentioned to Uncle Russell that I would like to make the trip again. He said that he would have to talk to Aunt Mitch.

Two or three days after our arrival in Portland the subject of my possible trip came up at supper. Surprisingly, it was approved by the Oregon group, contingent upon the approval of the New Hampshire group. Within two weeks plans were being made. I would go to Pacific Grove for three weeks then again I would take the bus cross country from San Francisco.

My freshman year finished successfully. We had a numerical grading system, A's were ones, B's were twos, and so on. I had five ones and two twos. One of the twos was in English, something about using too many commas. I didn't win a race but I came in second several times.

Pacific Grove was a good vacation place. I spent the first week in Carmel, with the two French ladies. A niece, also named Adrienne, was there for the week from Palo Alto. We spent time at Pebble Beach Country Club, putting on the practice green and had lunch in the dining room. The rest of the time we walked on the beach, and in town. We always seemed to end up at her cousin Renée's hobby shop. For some strange reason her Aunt Adrienne must have taken over a hundred pictures of us. The week passed quickly. She went back to Palo Alto and I to Pacific Grove. We corresponded for most of the summer.

I had about a week and a half left in P.G. Uncle Russell didn't want to start any experiments with me since there would no be time to derive any result. So he left me home. I went to see Jim who had now found new friends from school. Ann had a boy friend but went to the movie with me for old time's sake. I spent quite a bit of time in the drugstore looking at comic books since I couldn't bring them home.

There was a pocket book cover that really intrigued me. I knew that I couldn't buy it because I was too young, so when the druggist wasn't looking I slipped it under my shirt. Bought a comic book and left.

I went right to the beach, sat in the rocks and began reading "Mistress Glory". I kept looking behind me thinking that I had been seen stealing the book. I knew I was to be caught. I read half of the book, tucked it back under my shirt and went home to hide it under my mattress. I worried about that book half of the night. I had never stolen anything before and didn't like the feeling of being a thief. I hadn't been to church in over a year but I had learned what the priests had taught me well, the fear of God and the fear of hell and the difference between right and wrong.

My stomach stayed in a knot, I hardly ate any breakfast. Aunt Mitch said that I must be nervous over my upcoming trip. I agreed with her. I got the book and went back to the beach to finish it. That night the book seemed to burn a hole right through the mattress into me. I kept turning over to get comfortable. I had made up my mind way after midnight. I would go to the drugstore and give the book back to the druggist then take my punishment. That decision eased my mind and I went right to sleep. I ate a full breakfast and told Aunt Mitch I was going to visit Jim. It was true, I was going by his house.

The book still under my shirt, I walked in the drugstore full of good intentions. The druggist was busy filling a prescription as I wandered over to the books. I looked at the comics occasionally looking back at the druggist through the large mirror over the comic book rack. I felt the time had come to place the book back on the rack. It would be returned and I would feel fine even though I hadn't told the druggist of my transgression.

I picked up a comic book walked to the counter, paid my ten cents and started to walk out. The druggist looked at me and said smiling, "Thanks for bringing the book back, I felt that you would!" I was so ashamed. I looked down at my shoes on the way out and never went back into that store.

The three weeks were up and I was on the bus to San Francisco, I had to make a late evening connection east. We arrived in the middle of a rainstorm. I went inside trying to verify the departure time. I still had two hours so I sat on one of the wooden seats looking thoughtlessly at a book that I had been given for the trip. It was Kipling's "Kim".

A woman and her cute daughter were sitting opposite. The daughter and I eyed each other for awhile, I thought that she was about my age. I got up to go to the candy counter, within a minute she was buying gum beside me. We said, Hi to each other but that was it. I guess that I was more bashful than I thought.

Almost two hours later my bus was called; mom and daughter jumped up. Hurrah! They were to be on the same bus. I waited until they boarded than I got on and sat in the seat directly behind the girl. I put my suitcase away and kept "Kim" out.

We rode until daybreak when we stopped for breakfast. Since I was traveling by myself, mom asked me to join them for breakfast. I accepted immediately. Mary and I sat together throughout the days, but at night mom made her come back with her. Darn! We did manage to hold hands almost all day the third day and evening. They were from Concord, California going to Erie, Pennsylvania to visit grandparents. We separated in Pittsburgh, but not before we had each other's address and promised faithfully that we would write.

Journey Nine

Pacific Grove to Lancaster,
to Rochester to Portland

Chapter Twenty-one

They both met me at the bus station, mother shed a few tears; Wayne stood back and eventually shook my hand. Wayne had taught my mother to drive a blue 1939 Ford, for her commute to Lancaster. She drove to the house to show me what she had learned. If Aunt Mitch could do it, so could she!

The house had been painted and looked neater than when I had been there before. I went upstairs to my room and unpacked. At supper, Wayne told me proudly, that he had found me a job at a dairy. I would wash milk bottles in the morning and then work on the farm after I finished. It was six days a week from four thirty until dark through Friday, on Saturdays I would get off at noon. My salary was to be twenty-five dollars per week. Saturday afternoons and Sundays I could help him around "the place".

As a change of pace I went to the "Grange" to participate in vacation Bible school. I earned first place in comprehension and was awarded a Bible by the New Hampshire Bible Society. That seemed to bring me a lot of resentment from the local kids. Apparently receiving that Bible was a pretty big deal each summer, the results were in the newspaper. I had just arrived here and I "took it away" from them. I could tell this was going to be a great month.

One Saturday night Wayne piled us into the "Ford" to go to a movie called a drive-in, in Littleton, several miles away. We got lost and arrived just in time for the "Newsreel" so we ended up in the next to last row close to the rear exit. I have no recollection of the movie but I do remember that almost halfway through a handwritten note flashed on the screen over the movie. " Man here with other man's wife, husband at gate, leave by back!" Four cars went by us with lights out.

I had gotten the bottle washing system down well enough that I finished almost an hour faster than anyone ever had. Lucky me; I now had the chance to work longer in the silo. Chopped corn and other feed mixed with syrup and water was conveyered up forty or fifty feet to drop through the opening of the silo. Since I was the youngest I had the privilege of being inside to even the level of feed with a pitchfork. That mixture was continuously dropping on me. The second or third day the stuff was starting to ferment, heating up and emitting fumes that kept me lightheaded. Johnny the owner explained it, he said I "was plain drunk, that's what happened in there". I had to ride home in the back of the pickup and take my clothes off in the wood shed. Then I scrubbed in the tub for a half-hour. The next day would start all over.

I started wondering if my idea had been as good as I had thought it was in Oregon. My mother was working in town at the Drug Company; Wayne was working at the dairy, so we had just supper to talk. Those conversations consisted of please pass the potatoes or something as profound. On the other hand with the Moores we had an active mealtime conversation about events of the day, either theirs or mine; about music, the theater and sometimes even about politics.

Serge was in Rochester at the Eastman School of Music studying for his Master's in composition. Mother decided that since I was there with her, it would be a good time for us to go visit Serge. It had been a couple of years since we three had been together. I told her that I would go with her. We were to take the bus, but Wayne wouldn't hear of it. He decided that he would drive us. Mother could stay a week and he would return for her.

He dropped us off at the house where Serge was renting a room not far from school. The landlady let us in to wait for him since he was in class. Serge was really surprised. Mother had not contacted him to say we were coming. He gave us the bed and he slept on the floor. We had one dinner together in a small restaurant. Mother went to the room, and then Serge took me to a department store to meet his girlfriend. That was the total time he and I spent together.

Mother decided that she was going to stay for awhile. She went to look for a job since she didn't like the way that Serge was living. He was thin and needed a hair cut. She telephoned Wayne to tell him she would return later. I stayed in his room for a day and a half hardly going outside; finally I told myself that it was time to go.

I had a roundtrip ticket from Boston. Now I was in Rochester so we had to have the ticket changed to go to Pittsburgh. I didn't even see Serge before I left. Mother went with me to the bus station, told me to be careful cried a little and left. I hung out in the waiting room thinking there was a chance that Mary and her mother would be going back to California on the same bus, but that was not to be.

The constant hum of tires on asphalt almost put me to sleep, I started daydreaming. I felt sure that mother really wasn't happy. But what could I do? I certainly couldn't invite her to come with me. She and Aunt Mitch didn't get along. When I stopped to think about it I didn't have a place that I called home. I was fortunate that I had a nice place to live. Other kids said they were going home, I always said I was "going to the house". Anyway, she was the one who had rejected me. I was now fourteen years old, I had worked, and I even had a social security number so if I had to, I could really be on my own. But for now I would go back to Portland and see what the next year brought.

This traveling by myself was great stuff. I liked it! I guessed that I had come by it naturally. Both my mother and my father had traveled extensively for business as well as for pleasure. A well endowed sixteen-year-old girl and I sat together for a day or so but the attraction that Mary and I had felt wasn't there this time. In fact I sat next to this girl, name forgotten, and wondered when Mary and her mother were going back to Concord. She had been really cute, she smelled nice and she liked to hold hands. I would write to her as soon as I arrived in Portland.

My seat partner left the bus in Omaha and a man got on and sat next to me. We talked about odds and ends all day. He was from India and he began to tell me about elephants. The next day we were getting close to Salt Lake City when he reached in his bag and took out a package of photographs. He showed me one and asked what I thought of it? I said it was O.K. So he handed me the stack to look at. I leafed through them quickly, they were of men and women in various stages of undress practicing varied acts. I handed them back to him. Soon we stopped in a small town to get something to eat. I went to the restroom and this man showed up and went into a booth. He waited until I was washing my hands to try to get me to get in the booth with him. I ran out of there, hands still dripping. I found the driver and told him what had happened. He walked out to the bus, took the man's bag out of the overhead, put it on the loading dock and told him to catch another bus.

The driver sat me down to try to explain what had happened and to tell me to be very careful when I traveled alone. I thanked him and said that I had heard about things like that but had never been approached before. Certainly I would not talk with strangers, at least not strange men. Drivers changed in Salt Lake City and the rest of the trip was fine.

Journey Ten

Portland to Lancaster

Chapter Twenty-two

My sophomore year started well. I was still on the track team. Alex had found new friends during the summer. Mary and I corresponded even while I was infatuated with a quiet girl named Bernice. My second year of Spanish was as interesting as the first. A gorgeous auburn haired junior named Dolores hung around a lot for me to help her with her homework. Shirley wanted us to bake cookies at her house. Skeeter and I shot B.B.'s at Mary Beth's windows across the street, through our front door's "peek-out" port, as Aunt Mitch called it. His sister beat him up with a baseball bat.

Uncle Russell and I went back to Friday Harbor for Easter vacation. This time we visited the fort that had marked the boundary between the United States and Canada. It seems that in 1859 an American shot a pig that belonged to a British settler. That event started a boundary dispute that lasted twelve years, it was known as the Pig War. Both the United States and Canada occupied the island until William I of Germany, the arbitrator of the dispute awarded it and the entire San Juan Islands archipelago to the United States in 1872.

One Sunday Aunt Mitch told me to get ready we were going for a ride to the airport. We got in the old Nash, she had me sit in front and Uncle Russell in the back for a change. She finally explained why Uncle Russell didn't drive anymore. As a scientist his mind was too busy to concentrate on the road. A few years before he had been driving and thinking about an experiment when a boy on a bicycle came too far out into the street. Uncle Russell, not paying attention, struck the bicycle and killed the boy. He swore that from then on, he would never drive again.

The area around the airport was sparsely populated. Aunt Mitch stopped the car and told me to walk around the driver's side. She was going to give me my first driving lesson. That was great, but I had driven tractors and trucks on the farm the previous summer. She wanted me to have a learner's permit so that I could help her drive on the trips to California.

After driving for awhile we stopped in a parking lot and watched planes take off and land. I decided to forget the diplomatic service; this was what I wanted to do. We saw a sign saying Civil Air Patrol. I had heard that one of the boys in school had joined. I mentioned that I might be interested in joining. She was back behind the wheel. We drove on the grounds right to the CAP office where they were meeting on Sundays. I joined as a Cadet.

Back at the house, Uncle Russell said that it was time to start talking about college. I was doing well with my grades and I was expected to keep them up to qualify for a scholarship. I agreed with that. Then he said I would go to the University of Portland and major in marine biology. I told him that I enjoyed working on experiments with him but I wasn't sure what I wanted to do for the rest of my life. I wanted something a little more exiting. That statement must have made him snap. He said "science was exiting. There was a discovery just waiting for the right person to identify it". He then went on to say that I "was no longer grateful, and if I expected him to help me with college it would be under their terms". I knew Uncle Russell had an occasional glass of wine but I had never seen him or heard him like this. I looked helplessly at Aunt Mitch who was warming super; she conveniently faced the other way.

I had been with them almost four years, I really did care for them and I was grateful for everything they had done for Serge and me. Without their help we would probably still be in France. Not that being in France was bad but I loved being in the United States. This was now my country! One of mother's friends had once said that he would pay my way to the University of Michigan, but only if I became a rubber chemist. We had both said no thank you.

I wondered why life had to be a constant compromise. One had to make concessions in order to get something. Why not just give a gift for the sake of giving or if you couldn't do that, then don't bother. That type of gift really wasn't a gift; it was an exchange of goods for a feeling of personal satisfaction. It was almost like saying I'll write you off if you don't do what I want. One should have nothing to do with the other.

Why should I follow in his footsteps to be an good citizen? I had become intrigued by meteorology and felt that it was an interesting science and an honorable profession. But what the heck, I still had two full years of high school to make up my mind. Why did this come about today?

The following week when Aunt Mitch took me to get my learner's permit I brought up the past Sunday's discussion. She looked concerned and told me that Uncle Russell was worried about his health. He had to go on a salt free diet. I decided that I wouldn't loose any sleep over a college major right now. I still had a little over a month of school until final exams. Again I did well so there was no problem.

My mother had written to invite me to spend a month with them again that summer. I hesitated to show the letter to Aunt Mitch but she had received one at the same time, so she was prepared and said that it would be a good idea. She drove me to the bus station.

The bus trip was downright dull. We stopped in Cheyenne for lunch. A few days later, when I arrived in New York, I had to wait a few hours for my bus to Lancaster. I went on a tour bus for two hours. We drove by the Empire State Building and Grant's Tomb.

Wayne seemed genuinely pleased to see me this time. We arrived at the house before dark, and walked around the five acres to look at the new chicken house that he had added. They now had four thousand laying hens. But eggs were not making much money, he told me.

He showed me how we were going to clean the winter's collection of straw and droppings that had grown to a depth of ten or twelve inches. The smell of ammonia was overpowering. We would start the next day. That night, Wayne said that he had even started selling eggs from the milk truck he was driving for Johnny Fortin. He had to give Johnny ten cents commission for each dozen he sold from the truck. Money had been real tight, now my being there would help. My wages would go toward household expenses.

Mother had continued her correspondence with Ed and Uncle Abe during the last two years. He invited us to drive down to see them. Wayne arranged with his nephews, John and Peter, to take care of the hens while we were away.

Uncle Abe and Aunt Mae welcomed us. Uncle Abe took me to the factory to see everybody again. We went to the diner for lunch. Our waitress was no longer there, so I asked what happened to her. She had gone to New York to become a dancer.

Uncle Abe arranged for Wayne to meet a man from Maryland who owned a large tobacco farm. Some of his buildings, including three houses, needed renovations. He offered Wayne the job of overseeing the repairs. He would even furnish a house for us to live in. Wayne thought that it was too good to pass up. We went back to Lancaster to start liquidating the farm.

Wayne and mother bought a nineteen-foot travel trailer to hitch onto the back of the old "Ford". They arranged to auction the farm, the hens, and the furniture. They kept only what we could load in the trailer.

I asked what we were going to do with my cat "Tiger". Wayne said that we were definitely not taking it, and for me to take him to the woods and shoot him. I protested strongly. Someone had given him to me the first year we stayed there, when I was in the fifth grade. He had slept at my feet for almost a year and again each time that I had stayed in Lancaster. Since the war I had not been too interested in hunting or killing anything. I had seen enough death of people and animals.

Wayne told me to either go shoot him or he would. I asked when we were leaving for Maryland? He told me early the next morning. I tried to get Johnny to take Tiger. They had plenty of cats around their dairy barn so his father didn't want another. I thought of taking him to the woods to release him, but reasoned that he would probably starve. So just before dark I picked him up and took him to Wayne. I held tiger up, again asking to keep him. I would feed him as I had been doing anyway; he could sleep in my bed. The answer was the same. " No! Go shoot him." I held on to my Tiger, as I went in the trailer to get my twenty-two rifle. I tried to find a shovel to bury him, but there wasn't even a shovel left from the auction. I walked into the woods carrying him and the rifle.

I leaned the rifle against a tree and sat on a fallen log, holding the only pet that I had ever had of my own. I petted him while telling him what I was going to have to do, and that it was so he wouldn't suffer. He purred in my arms louder than I had ever hear him purr. I heard the car horn blow. It was meant for me to get this over with and come back to eat. I tried to place him down at my feet; he seemed to sense there was something wrong. He jumped back into my arms as I crouched beside him. Again I put him down, now with tears running down my face. He crouched under a small branch long enough for me to cock my rifle. He looked up at me, tilting his head quizzically as I brought the barrel behind his head. I closed my eyes and pulled the trigger. It had been a clean shot. I broke down and cried like I hadn't cried since I found out my father was never coming back. I used a piece of a branch to dig a shallow grave, then covered him with as many rocks as I could find to keep scavengers away. My relationship with Wayne would never the same.

Journey Eleven

Lancaster to La Plata, Maryland
to Shelton, Connecticut

Chapter Twenty-three

The trip to Maryland went from a blur to a haze. I was angry with Wayne, but even more enduringly, I was sickened from his demand. We stopped overnight in Connecticut and left early the following day. The trip was planned for us to go through New York City. Wayne had never towed a trailer and was extremely apprehensive. He did all right, and we spent the night in a roadside turnoff. We pulled into La Plata, Maryland early in the afternoon.

We had been told to go to an auto dealership that the farm owner also owned. He took us right out to the farm to set up the trailer. It seemed that he had rented the house that had been offered to us. That was the good part. Everything else went downhill. The trash would have to be shoveled out of the buildings just to see what repairs they would need. There was no electricity, and the plumbing had to be completely redone.

There was still almost a month before the beginning of school. Wayne drafted me to do the shoveling, as well as all of the other unpleasant tasks. I understood the situation; I was the kid! During my real down days, I managed to remind myself that I could have been dead. So buck up!

Mother told me that she had written the Moores to tell them that I would not be returning that year. I thought, thanks for discussing it with me! She said Wayne would need me to help with the repairs. I said that I was planning on finishing school and asked if he expected me to drop out? The answer was not clear. I asked how the Moores felt? Mother said they thought that it might be better if I just stayed in Maryland.

I didn't understand their reasoning. We had planned some of the events for the fall. Uncle Russell and I had started to work on ancient Greek. He was familiar enough with it that he taught me for almost six months. We still had two or three months to finish the book. We had started visiting some of the museums in and around Portland. We were going back to Friday Harbor at Easter. They had planned on my college. That might have been the straw. He and I had the conversation about my major. I was aware that he wasn't pleased but had no idea that he had decided to write me off. Even then I demonstrated a lot of respect, disagreement maybe, but still with respect. There was no doubt that I didn't show much affection. Still he wasn't the kind of person that fostered affection.

I was hurt. I would do all right, but I was hurt. It wasn't long ago that they had adopted me. It seemed that I was being un-adopted. Probably because I had a mind of my own.

I registered as a junior at La Plata high school. We now had cold water and toilet facilities, but still no hot water. I began using the showers in the gym for my daily ablutions.

School went well, but I couldn't participate in any sport, since I had to work. The bus brought me back within walking distance of the trailer. If I thought my days were dragging, I had to put myself in my mother's place. She stayed in that nineteen-foot trailer all day every day. She began sketching, mostly from memory, since all we had around us were empty fields. She kept saying that she would go out of her mind just sitting there without her books. She joined a book club. She told Wayne that she would go without dessert, but she had to have books. I read every book she received. My favorite was "The Iron Mistress", the story of Jim Bowie and his knife.

I enjoyed the idea of being with my mother, but I certainly didn't enjoy the physical part of this togetherness. I told her that we needed to have a serious conversation, very soon. There were issues that I felt we needed to resolve. First the trailer was just too small for the three of us. I was still sleeping on a door with folded blankets for a mattress, raised off the floor by four piles of bricks. I felt sure that the farm owner was taking advantage of Wayne. I didn't know what he was getting paid but I didn't think it was much. I found out the store where we bought our food was owned by the same man. The prices were much higher than in town.

I told her that there was no sense in her being stuck in that type of hovel. She was smart and talented. She had given up opportunities to live in mansions, even since we arrived in this country. As far as I was concerned, if Wayne wanted to stay there he could, but I felt that she and I could do a lot better on our own. She cried and agreed with me. But this was her fourth husband so she would support him any way that she could.

It made no difference that I was on the honor roll. Living like we were living was the common denominator. We were looked down upon, I found out we had been called "sharecroppers". I wasn't familiar with that term, but apparently in tobacco country, it meant you were not very high on the social scale.

Gratefully, I did have two friends, a girl, Ann and her brother Lynn. He was a senior, and had a car. So he and Ann gave me a ride back to the trailer almost every day. She and I became somewhat of a couple. She had cute freckles and a walk that turned all the boys' heads. She lived almost in Waldorf, the next town north on Highway 301.

Unknown to me, mother wrote to Uncle Abe. Just before Christmas vacation mother took the car and drove me to the bus stop, with my things packed in an old duffel bag.

Late that night I got off the bus in Derby right across the Housatonic River from Shelton. Uncle Abe met me and took me back to the house on the hill. Aunt Mae had died earlier. We had not even been told. We had a snack of pickled herring in cream and mazzo's.

I went up to the luxurious tiled shower and soaked until my hands and feet turned to prunes. Uncle Abe said that we would be fine. We could batch it. I would prepare breakfast and he would do supper. A housekeeper came in twice a week for the laundry and cleaning.

After school I went to see Al, the foreman of Uncle Abe's basket factory. I was given a job bending basket handles, next to another boy named Bob. We were paid piecework as an incentive. Once, when Uncle Abe and I were walking around the factory, he told me "Work smart and you won't have to work as hard". We took advantage of his advice and streamlined the process. It had been done the same way for ten years or more without question or change. We became so adept, that the rate per rack was dropped. My piecework rate converted to an outstanding $2.56 per hour. Others who had been there for years were still at $1.75, so it was creating problems. Some of the older workers started dropping hints about wanting us to slow down; we were making them look bad.

Bob and I took that as a challenge and started looking again on how to increase our production. We rearranged the racks and the position of the bending jig again and increased the production even more. Two other workers usually bent handles during the time we were in school. Our production became so good that we became the only ones to bend handles, just part time.

I was almost last to wash up one evening when three of the men, took me in the restroom, stuck my head down into a commode and flushed it. "That's for not paying attention", I was told.

They seemed to know that I wouldn't say anything to Uncle Abe. And they were right, I didn't. But I couldn't slow down. Strangely, the following Monday, Al transferred to the tool part of the factory.

I had to operate a drill press for a few weeks. I cleaned up around my machine and rearranged the wooden cases and again the production began to increase. So Charlie, the plant engineer had me assigned to him. We spent the next couple of months reviewing each position in production. We were able to let some of the people sit down instead of standing and even increase their production. One middle-aged lady had stood there for years. Her legs became so swollen by afternoon that she stayed in pain most of the time. I rearranged her workstation and brought her a stool. She sat down for a week; her piece count increased and her legs didn't hurt as much. She brought me a rhubarb pie, hugged me and said that she would love me forever. Well Mary, I still remember you.

Bob and I were friends outside of work also. He, his cousin Bill, and one of my neighbors, Dave, became the Three Musketeers to my D'Artagnan. We went everywhere together. We raced cars on back roads. We got somebody to buy our beer and went to the beach. We would pool our change, fill up the '52 Packard that Uncle Abe let me drive and go to New York for a piece of pie and a cup of coffee. We dressed in suits wherever we went. It made us look older. We even went ice skating in Rockefeller Plaza in suits. We went to the Waldorf-Astoria to see the General Motors "Motorama". As we came out of the ballroom we stumbled onto a wedding reception in one of the party rooms. A glass of champagne and a couple of canapés later, a man we took to be the father of the bride smilingly, but through gritted teeth told us to "Get to hell out, and don't come back, or I'll call the cops!" We went back to school bragging that we had been thrown out of the Waldorf-Astoria.

The four of us spent the first month of the summer bumming around together. We were going to be seniors in the fall and were pretty hot stuff. I bought my clothes at Saul Steinman's, with a discount. All I had to do in exchange was tell the guys at school where to buy their clothes. That was a deal!

Mr. Steinman had an older son Mark, who was out of college, but was not too good with money. So he asked if I would go to Miami Beach for ten days, all expenses paid to keep an eye on his son. It took me about three seconds to agree. Apparently he had already talked to Uncle Abe about it because when I asked his permission, he said yes. I had some vacation time due from the factory so I took that.

We got in his 1952 "Chevy" and headed south. We stopped in Waldorf and went to the house of a girl I had befriended before my departure for Connecticut. Her mother was single so she and Mark got along famously; beer and all. Daughter and I took the car and met some of the kids from school. The next morning we continued down Highway 301 to Smithfield, North Carolina. Ann and her family had just moved there after school. When we arrived in town I called her house. They were having a family reunion. So she invited us. We spent the night in her parent's house.

Miami Beach was great. We checked into the hotel. Mark said he was tired from driving so he was going to sleep for awhile. I went to the beach for two or three hours and promptly got sunburned. When I returned to the hotel Mark had finished his nap, he was at the pool with two women who had to have been ten years older. They were buying Tom Collins with little umbrellas for him, so he was happy.

I met a girl from Chicago, she and her family were visiting relatives. She invited me to lunch at their house. Her father owned a string of clothing stores in Chicago. This girl was the fourth of five daughters. After a drink or two he took me aside to tell me that he had a policy of buying each of his new sons in law a clothing store as a wedding present. I accepted the fact that I looked older. I was never asked my age when Mark and I went into a bar. But I told the father that I had to finish college before I did anything like that. I couldn't very well tell him that his daughter didn't meet my standards. (Whatever they were at that time) He seemed to appreciate my position and the day was pleasant.

That episode reinforced another bit of advice that Uncle Abe had once given me. Which was "Don't ever go out with anyone that you would not be proud to bring home or to marry". Great advice!

We made it back to Shelton without any mishaps. Mark was happy, his father was pleased and I had a great vacation. It was time for my senior year to begin.

Chapter Twenty-four

Serge had found a job working for "Eastman-Kodak". His graduate work was going fairly well, but somehow he ended up in the United States Air Force. He was stationed at Sampson Air Force Base in Geneva, New York. After basic training he was assigned to the band squadron.

He was one of, if not the, composer for that band. He was assigned to compose a multimedia piece (orchestral, dance and voice) commemorating the fiftieth anniversary of powered flight. He entitled it " Conquest of the Air". I received an invitation from the Commanding General of the base to attend and to be seated in a select area. I took advantage of the invitation and stayed at the General's house. It seemed that Serge and the General's daughter were engaged. "Conquest of the Air" was performed to much acclaim on November 7th, 1953. Those few days of parties, and the salutes I received coming in and out of the base gate while driving the general's car, whetted my appetite for military life.

I went back to Shelton with a lot on my mind. Our mother had also attended the performance. I tried to talk to her, almost to no avail. She did say that she and Wayne had decided to leave Maryland and to come live in Connecticut. They bought a small piece of property in Oxford. Wayne was going to get a job in construction and he would build a house in his spare time, meanwhile they would live in the trailer until the house was closed in.

I realized that she was going to stay with him, so I offered to help on weekends. I said that I had gotten pretty good with tools. She agreed that we would talk about it.

Uncle Abe and I went to New Haven to visit friends of his who were on the board at Yale. My grades had dropped off a little but my three-year average was still where it needed to be for admission to that venerated institution. I had no interest in football, I still liked track but I had not participated in over a year. Uncle Abe and his friend decided that I should join the fencing team, my European background would make me a natural. The son of the friend was a highly regarded member of that team who took me under his wing for the day. We went to his practice studio. There, he placed an epée in my hand and began to explain the fundamentals. I was in!

On the way back home Uncle Abe told me that he had been seeing a lady for a few months and they were getting married. It would not change anything as I would continue living at the house with them until it was time for me to go to Yale. Then I could major in business and work with his son Raymond in the factory. He wanted to expand and that would give him additional management that he could trust. I thought to myself that I had seen enough shouting matches between Uncle Abe and Raymond while running the business, I wasn't sure that I wanted to be involved in all of that.

Halloween came and the three musketeers and d'Artagnan struck. We piled into Uncle Abe's Packard with a hand pump type, fire extinguisher. We went to Derby and began to cruise, looking for likely victims. Bill and Dave were in the back seat pumping. Bob had the nozzle hidden under his wrist with the passenger window down and I drove. We would lure an unsuspecting victim to the car and then pump water to spray an area that might cause the most embarrassment.

This was so much fun that we drove by the waiting ticket line at the movie. We wet all the girls and a few of the boys. That had been so successful that I drove around the block again. The pumpers were pumping as hard as they could, the nozzle guy was aiming and laughing until he yanked the nozzle back into the car yelling "Stop, stop". The headliner and the seat already wet I looked to the right. Standing on the edge of the sidewalk was a policeman wearing winter blues full of white flour-paste patches. They came from the younger kids who would fill socks with flour and run by the beat cop, smacking him with the sock, leaving a nice halo of flour on blue wool. We came along with the water to turn all that flour into a paste.

He managed to pull his whistle and got us to stop. I thought of running but everyone in this town, and in Shelton, knew that car. That was one of the disadvantages of living in a small town. The officer climbed in and said something about the "junior fire department". We drove to the police station where they confiscated the tank. We walked in the entrance and the desk sergeant took one look at his beat cop and began laughing. Our friend in blue was not amused, he ushered us into a small interrogation room. There we sat and sat, probably for an hour or more. We were saying all the right things, with proper humility, just in case anyone was listening. Bill raised his voice with" If we ever get out of here, I'm going straight home and staying". Probably another half-hour later, the sergeant came in asking for our driver's licenses. He started with the driver, asking me whose car that was and who I was. When I told him he shook his head, and went to Bob, he asked if his dad was so and so? Bob said "yes sir". He went to Bill who quickly said he was Bob's cousin. The sergeant shook his head again and looked at Dave's license. He asked if his dad was so and so? It was Dave's turn to say "yes sir".

The sergeant threw the licenses on the table and told us to "get out of his town", if he saw that car in town again that night, he was putting us in jail. Bill asked for his tank back, the sergeant told him to have his father come pick it up the following week. As far as I know that tank is probably somewhere around the police station today. I know he didn't tell his dad. We went to Bob's house, parked the Packard, and told his mother what had happened. She became starry-eyed and said wistfully that she wished she had been there. We said, "great, can we borrow the Studebaker?" We borrowed his dad's car and pump then went back to Derby. We rationalized that we were not in the Packard, so it would be all right.

Wayne was making good headway on the stone foundation. I was going there on weekends to help mix mortar and carry stones. We went up with the outside walls and roof. One Saturday Wayne had to work at his job site.

I bought a bottle of some type of red wine without a request for identification, and went to the trailer. Mother was painting so I watched her for a little while. I gently took the paintbrush from her hand and sat it down on her easel.

I poured each of us a glass of wine and said it was time to talk again. I had figured out that my being away had two main causes. First, Wayne wasn't too wild about my living with them for whatever reason. Second, I felt that mother wanted me to have some sort of privileged upbringing. If indeed, this was part of her motivation and she really wanted me around, but was sacrificing our being together for my comfort, I appreciated it, but she had made a big mistake. I told her that I had lost one parent eleven years before, and I had looked forward to spending my youth before college as at least a partial family. I didn't need all the comforts and the status. I was smart enough and industrious enough that I would have all those, when I went out on my own.

I had learned a lot in the short time in La Plata. Other people's opinions didn't mean as much to me. Of course it could be that the tide had turned, I was now envied instead of being looked down upon. I wondered about that. I was still the same person, just in a different environment. I realized however, that I was more interested in the affection of my mother and the exchange of words and ideas as opposed to the physical comforts.

Serge knew that he had been discarded and I was feeling the same way. We only had a few months before I graduated and left. "Please think about this". I told her Uncle Abe was getting married and I felt that I should be moving out. He had said it was all right but I didn't think his new wife would want a teenager around.

Two or three weeks later I moved into the basement of the one room house and helped Wayne as often as he was there. We built the interior rooms and I moved upstairs. He and I still had a reserved relationship.

Uncle Abe seemed relieved that I had moved out. The wedding was nice. I met the bride briefly. He was in his early seventies and she was in her late sixties. She had two or three sons and several grandchildren just about my age. They seemed to have taken over the house. One day before the end of school, Uncle Abe had me meet him at the old diner after work He put his arm around my shoulders looked down at the counter shaking his head, and said " Boy! I made a terrible mistake. Now I can't even help you with college anymore." I was taken back a little. Uncle Abe was the only one who had offered to do something without seeming to expect something else in exchange.

Even though, in our last conversation at Yale, I had the feeling that he would require me to major in business because that was part of the deal, we really never discussed it. The subject was tabled; to be brought up at a later date.

I felt sorry for him. He had paid a tremendous price for feminine companionship. He was wealthy but unhappy. In his attempt to please his new family he had given up his pride, maybe even his masculinity.

Final exams were finished. We had the usual elections for class everything wonderful. Surprisingly I won three categories. My "Argus" annual signatures "lucked" me into eternity. Senior banquet was great. A girl that I never dated and I got together, by class design. Her boy friend was in college and I had really never gotten serious about any girl in school, so the busybodies in the class paired us up. We spent the night parked by the river, literally crying in our left over beer, about life in general. She had not gone out with anyone locally her entire senior year and now her boy friend had just dumped her. As for me, my college plans were flushed down the drain. On top of that we bemoaned the fact that we had not gotten together earlier of our own volition, without class meddling.

She went to sleep on my shoulder around three o'clock. I was wide-awake. My mind was racing. We only had a few days before graduation. I had not applied for a scholarship; I had not even applied for admission anywhere else. I was so sure of Uncle Abe and my acceptance at Yale. I had made no backup plan. The acceptance was still there, but the money wasn't.

Uncle Russell came to mind; we had corresponded from time to time during the previous year, just general topics and nothing personal. I knew that they had been hurt, when I didn't return. I was too proud to go back and ask favors from that quarter. I was certain that I could get into the teacher's college on short notice. My grades were good. But there was such a stigma about going there. The joke was, if you couldn't get in anywhere else, you could always go to teacher's college. They would take anybody; after that you could become a teacher. This, undoubtedly, was not a fair characterization of the school or of the students.

I thought of my mother and her unhappy marriage to someone who was unable to challenge her mind. She had struggled so hard for the three of us to come to this country to be free, and soon after reaching it, she impatiently orchestrated her own confinement. Perhaps it was not as much in the physical sense but certainly in the mental.

She was so hungry for knowledge and mental exercises. She volunteered for jury duty lasting six months, then presented her husband with her summons to show that she had to leave the house daily. She was tired during those days. Her day started by taking the bus to New Haven, every morning at six oclock. She seemed happier than I had seen her in years.

It had been a long time since I had engaged my father in a conversation. I could see the darkness turn to lighter shades of gray in the east. I realized that I had been awake all night. My thoughts were fleeting from one topic to another. My shoulder was numb from Terry's head, her hair smelled like lilies of the valley. I wanted to know if he might be alive somewhere... Surely, he could not really have died... He would be back... Her hands were long and slender; she should be a concert pianist...

All our acquaintances had had such an impact on our lives... We had been dependent without really contributing. We had been accepted as friends, even adopted as family... What had we done in return? Not much! We owed a lot to many people.

The sun was just rising through the trees across the river, lighting not just the dawn, but also illuminating my way. My direction was clear and I had made up my mind.

Terry began to stir slightly, smiling up at me. She asked if I had slept? I told her no that I was just thinking. Terry knew nothing of my history, in fact no one did. I was tempted to tell her about it but I resisted. We went to the diner for a cup of coffee and a Danish. Other seniors had the same idea. We all sat around for awhile. I took Terry home. We kissed, almost desperately, knowing that we would never see each other again.

I telephoned Serge the day after my graduation. I was still seventeen but that would change in September. I had traveled many journeys during the previous eleven years. I had relied on others for lodging, for food and even the price of the journeys.

Now I was embarking on a new journey. It really was not freedom. I had decided there was no such true state. But in my view, I was free; free to go on with the rest of my life, in my own way.

I would start my declaration of freedom by joining the Air Force. This was by my own choice, on my terms, a means to partially repay my family's debt to these giving people and to this great country...

Now, really, my home...

Afterword

The fate of Gerard Gyula Geller, prisoner Number 6612, was not discovered until October of 1996.

He and others, were imprisoned in the Fort de Romainville, transferred to Compiegne and then to Drancy in preparation for deportation to the east. On February 11, 1943 he and 997 other Jews of different nationalities, and of all ages, were loaded on convoy number 47 to Auschwitz, Poland.

The train arrived on February 13, 1943, four months to the day of his betrayal and arrest in Paris.

One hundred forty three (143) men and fifty-three (53) women were selected as workers. The remaining souls in the convoy were immediately sent to the gas chambers.

Gerard Geller, with the proper birthplace and birth date, appeared on the manifest of Convoy #47. As a young man he suffered from tuberculosis and had one lung partially removed. He would have been deemed unfit for labor; therefore it has to be assumed that he was not selected as a worker.

This information was discovered through research conducted from the archives of the Holocaust Memorial Museum in Washington, DC by my nephew, Feréol de Gastyne. After fifty-three years of not knowing, I am grateful!

Louise Geller Norman is ninety-five years old, a resident in a nursing home, suffering from advanced Alzheimer's disease. Serge de Gastyne succumbed to coronary heart disease in 1992. Wayne Norman passed away in 1996.

ORDER FORM

Fax Orders: (601) 542-0114
Telephone orders: Call Toll Free: 1(888) 844-9922
Please have your Visa/ Master Card Ready
Postal Orders:

Ilrea Publishing
P.O. Box 123
Magnolia, MS 39652-0123, USA
Tel: (601) 542-5793

Please Send Me ________
Copies of JOURNEYS to FREEDOM by Guy Geller
Company Name: ______________________________

Name: ______________________________________

Address: ____________________________________

City: ______________ State: ____ ZIP: __________

Telephone: ____________________

Book Cost: $22.95
Sales Tax: Please add 7.00 % tax for Books Shipped to Mississippi addresses.
Shipping: $ 3.50 for first book and
$2.00 for each additional book.

Payment: Check [ ] Visa/Master Card [ ]

Card Number: __________________ Exp. Date: ______

Name on Card: ______________________________

Guy Geller's France during his journeys and concealment from 1942 to 1946.

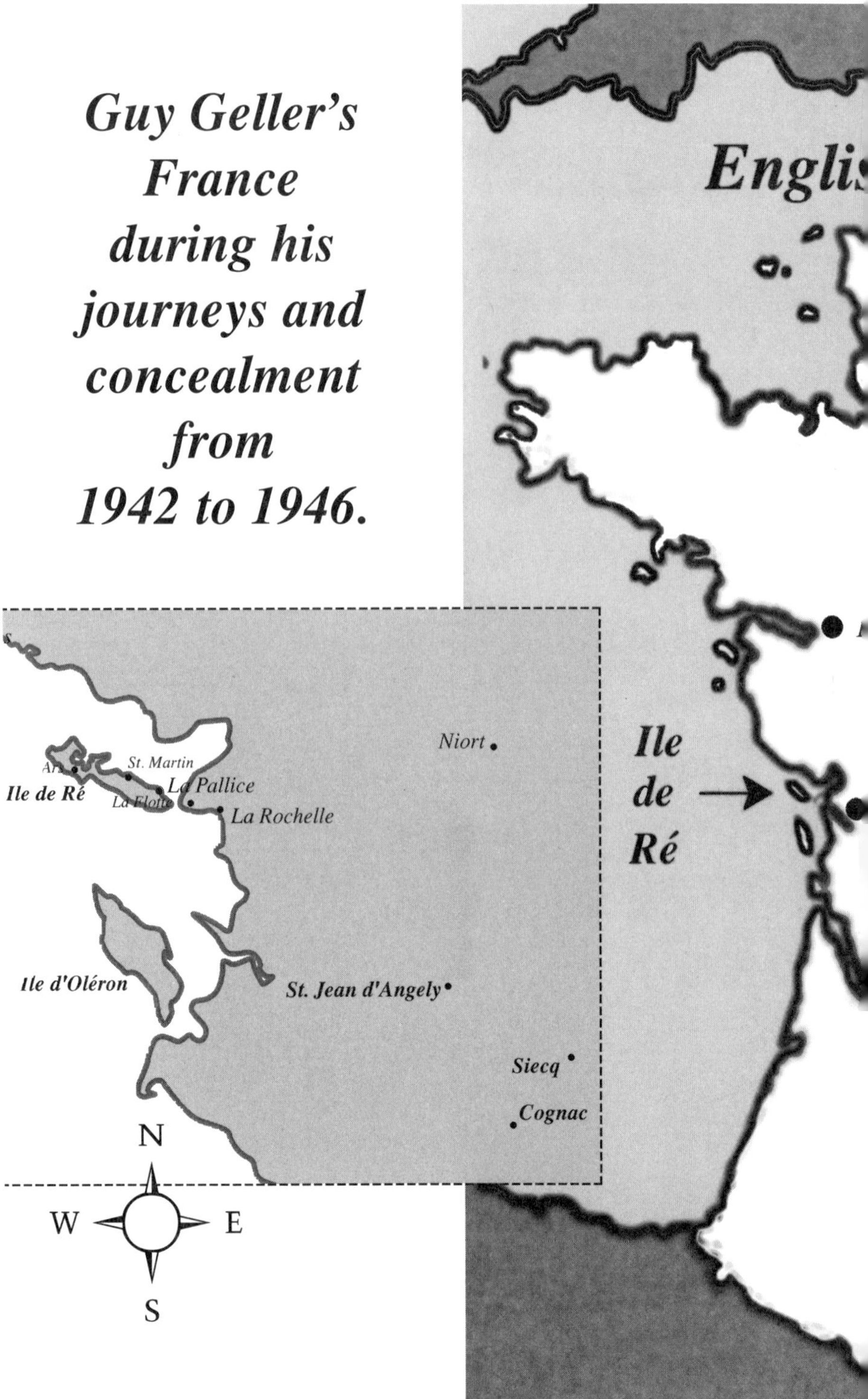